GOD
I WANT TO DANCE WITH YOU

BUT THIS TIME I WANT YOU TO LEAD

KAREN SEYMORE PORTMAN

God I Want to Dance with You: But This Time I Want You to Lead

Copyright© 2020 Karen Seymore Portman

All rights reserved. This book is protected under the copyright laws of the United States of America. This book may not be copied or reprinted for commercial gain or profit. The use of short quotations or occasional page copying for personal or group study is permitted and encouraged. Permission will be granted upon request. All emphases within quotations are the author's addition.

 Published by Final Step Publishing

P.O. Box 1447

Suffolk, VA 23439

www.finalsteppublishing.com

For Worldwide Distribution

Cover Design by Todd R. Simpson

Interior Design by Anno Domini Press

www.AnnoDominiPress.com

ISBN: 978-1-7342371-5-3

DEDICATION

"The Spirit of the Lord GOD is upon Me, because the LORD has anointed Me to preach good tidings to the poor; He has sent Me to heal the brokenhearted, to proclaim liberty to the captives, and the opening of the prison to those who are bound; To proclaim the acceptable year of the LORD, and the day of vengeance of our God; to comfort all who mourn, to console those who mourn in Zion, to give them beauty for ashes, the oil of joy for mourning, the garment of praise for the spirit of heaviness; that they may be called trees of righteousness, the planting of the LORD, that He may be glorified."
(Isaiah 61:1-3)

This book is dedicated to all who desire to be free to experience and live life to the fullest by faithfully serving the One who can make it all possible. It is to those who long to honestly say, "I'm in love with You, God. Thank You for sending Your Son to die for me because now I know that the truth really does make me free!"

SPIRITUAL ENDORSEMENT

First, let me say that Karen is God's lover. Please note I did not say a lover of God but rather God's lover. I believe as you journey with Karen through each chapter of her book you will conclude with me that she has chosen to give herself fully to the One she loves who is the One who loves her. Each chapter tells of self-discovery, referencing the daily norms of life and the expectations she placed upon herself and others. She shares her life obstacles and experiences as they begin to take on new, revelatory meaning.

It is my pleasure to endorse, "God, I Want to Dance with You." As you read this book you will see how the Spirit of God will give you eyes to see what you did not see before. This new understanding will create within you a desire to dance with God. As an apostolic, prophetic leader and a strategist with strong revelatory gifting, I am not surprised by Karen's ability to take her life experiences and see beyond the natural to see God's vision and purpose for her life. Dance, Karen, dance!

Apostle (Dr.) Peggy Scott

Fellowship Around the Word Church (founder), Franklin, VA and Peggy Scott Ministries, an apostolic and prophetic network

CONTENTS

Dedication iii
Spiritual Endorsement v
Introduction - The Motivation 1
Chapter 1 - Picture Perfect 5
Chapter 2 - The Fictitious Life 9
Chapter 3 - Alone at Last 13
Chapter 4 - I Want to Be Free 19
Chapter 5 - The Restoration Process 25
Chapter 6 - The Soul Closet 29
Chapter 7 - The Beasts in the Basement 33
Chapter 8 - Push Past the Pain 39
Chapter 9 - Truth Hurts, But It Heals 45
Chapter 10 - A Blessing in the Wilderness 49
Chapter 11 - A Spiritual Tune-Up in the Wilderness 57
Chapter 12 - Take the Plunge 63
Chapter 13 - The Mountaintop Experience 67
Chapter 14 - Pregnant with a Promise 73
Chapter 15 - The Other Side of Through 77
Chapter 16 - Sweet Surrender 83
Chapter 17 - The Dance 87
Closing Thoughts 91
Other Publications 97
About the Author 99

INTRODUCTION
The Motivation

I didn't realize I had so many distractions in my life. How could I? Everything I was involved in needed to be done, or at least I thought so. Little did I know that even though those actions needed to be done, they didn't have to be done by me. It was sometime later that I realized it was my need to be needed that was driving me. It was a need that came from other deep-rooted issues in my life.

Time and again God was trying to get my attention. The more I received instructions from Him, the busier I became with the cares of life that I refer to as subtle distractions. Though I prayed, I didn't spend as much time with the Lord as I should have. I was too busy doing things.

Because of His deep love for me, He sent others along my path to tell me about my distractions. I started receiving messages from various friends saying things such as, "God is really trying to talk to you and you have not had time to really listen," or "You are really distracted and you need to get away and spend time with Him." Some even sent me on paid getaways as His way to get my attention.

I believe the last straw was the morning I woke up praying. He reminded me of the story about Mary and Martha in Luke 10:38-42. I love that story. I opened my Bible to read it, beaming at first because I thought of myself, at that time, as a Mary. However, what I heard was something different. Very quiet and gentle, as a loving Father, I heard the Spirit say, "And right now, you are Martha."

That was a shock to me, and I was deeply saddened. The beaming pride I had suddenly turned to sadness. It wasn't because Martha was a bad person; it's just not the depiction I wanted for myself and certainly not where I wanted to be at that moment. I went into my living room and cried before the Father. I was ready at last to sit at His feet and listen to the instructions that could only come from the One who knows me and truly loves me.

Through a lot of fasting, prayer and the power of His Word, the Holy Spirit began to show me things about myself to break the strongholds that had taken root and grown in my life. I saw doors that needed to be closed, wounds that needed to be healed, and trust that needed to be restored. It was through my brokenness that healing could begin and restoration could take place. It was then that I decided to start the process of ridding myself of needless distractions and draw closer to the Lord so I could move towards my destiny. The closer I drew to Him, the more visions He began to show me.

According to Webster's College Dictionary, emotions are defined as "any of the feelings of joy, sorrow, fear, hate, love, etc." With a definition as broad as that, I believe it's safe to say that all of us experience both positive and negative emotions. Let's take a moment to deal with the negative ones.

The fact may be that we are struggling with something in our lives. It could be a painful memory from our past or a current situation that continues to play like a movie in our minds. It could be the traumatic affects or the feelings of growing up in what we thought was a dysfunctional family compared to other families we knew. We may be feeling unloved, rejected, cast out, lonely, or any other negative emotions. All this comes as part of living.

The truth is we don't have to stay on the roller coaster ride with our negative emotions by accepting the lies from situations brought into our lives. The lie leads us to believe that it's just the way we are or the way we'll always be; however, the Word of God leads us to the truth. Let's face it, pain doesn't feel good but if we allow God to heal us, He will unwrap us gently. He knows how much we can bear. Jesus came to set the captives free, and it's up to us to grab hold of that promise and allow Him into our heart to do the work.

Becoming emotionally whole is a process that can sometimes take years. But if we ask God to reveal the root cause of our issues and allow the truth of His Word to unravel us, we'll be set free from that torment and pain forever! Knowing the truth is a step towards freedom (John 8:31-32). Then, we will begin to take our thoughts captive with the Word (2 Corinthians 10:5). We must grab hold of the truth and rid ourselves of the chains of captivity. The power of God will move us into the fullness of everything He promised to us to reach our destiny.

Satan's job is to rob, to kill and to destroy us, but Jesus came to give us life and life more abundantly (John 10:10). Are you ready for the abundant life? I know that I am. Let's start by saturating ourselves in the Word of God so we can know what it says about living the abundant life. Then follow that up by speaking the Word and believing the Word. It doesn't mean that we won't experience pain, disappointments and probably some setbacks; however, we will be better equipped to handle them through the Word of God, and the results will be everlasting!

This book was inspired and written by the Holy Spirit and is not an autobiography. However, I will share a few of my personal experiences with the Lord, along with other examples, in hopes that it will bring freedom. I pray that you are blessed as the Holy Spirit ministers to you. Enjoy the journey.

I am gracefully broken, forever.

Karen Seymore Portman

CHAPTER 1
Picture Perfect

Have you read, heard or know of someone who appears to have themselves together and to have everything they could possibly need? Have you wished for one moment you could be like them, or at least have half of the success they had so you wouldn't have to struggle so much? Don't let what you see or read fool you. Some of the very ones you are wishing you could swap places with are miserable. Just because we see people with success, financial status, an active social life, and perhaps even a family does not mean they don't have problems. Some are very candid about them, and yet there are many who hide them behind their success. The bottom line is, we all deal with something.

For a moment, picture this: All heads turned when the couple entered the room. She looked as if she stepped right out of a fashion magazine. Her hair was neatly cut, her make-up was flawless and her nails were neatly manicured. Professionally dressed, she walked with confidence in her high-heeled shoes. Even though his arm was linked in hers, it was apparent to all present that she could hold her own if she needed to. He was also considered a good catch. He was well known by many and had the personality to "work a room." They both could have been on the cover of a magazine featuring happy couples.

Their smiles lit up the room. Their soft laughter to even the silliest joke made those in attendance feel comfortable. They walked in sync with each other. They greeted people they knew with a friendly hug and shook hands with many. They smiled and said, "happy" as the photographer flashed the camera. Little did those in attendance know that it was really a facade. Photographers can take a picture that lasts, but after the camera's flash, life returns.

Does this scene sound familiar? Isn't this like a nice portrait? We can be touched up to remove all the flaws but it's just a picture. We can frame family portraits with everyone posing and smiling picture-perfect; however, outside of the framed portrait, there is a real family feud going on, sometimes from several generations back. While looking at the framed picture, no one would notice that behind the smiles quarrelling was going on. What is really behind the masks we wear?

Allow me to share a story about a woman who needed healing from people who had hurt her. She cried many nights that left her pillow wet. She pondered and asked, "Why? What did I do to deserve this? Why did this have to happen to me? Why am I going through this?" She felt rejected, unloved and alone.

During times like this we could find ourselves asking God, "Where are You? You said You would never leave nor forsake me, but I'm not feeling Your presence right now." However, when people asked her how she was doing, her response was always, "I'm blessed" or "I'm fine," with a warm and friendly smile that was picture-perfect. She said it so much that she started to believe what she was saying, yet her pain kept getting buried deeper and deeper. One might say she had a smile that was painted on.

Suddenly there appeared to be a ray of sunshine. The agony was replaced with what seemed to be new hope and a fresh beginning. Soon her days were filled with exciting things that kept her busy and her mind occupied on other things. She was involved with taking care of her child, working full-time, managing the home, volunteering at her child's school and within the community, as well as the multiple church ministries and activities. She thought that was "the life." That was until her child grew up, and her busy assignments came to an abrupt close. The tears started again. The painful past resurrected itself right before her eyes.

She cried a lot during this time. No one, not even those close to her, knew about her sleepless nights or her inner pain because of the mask she wore. This went on for years without her ever knowing and acknowledging that she had problems that were deeply rooted because of pain she had buried. Being a Christian, she was supposed to have it all together. Instead, she had a hard time "keeping it real," not only with others but with herself. She continued hiding more behind her many masks.

At home she put on her everything-is-alright mask. At church she put on her praise-the-Lord-God-is-good mask. On the job she had on her happy mask. But inside she was hurting and didn't know it. Because she had been that way for so long, she accepted it as normal. She found self-worth as a caretaker and nurturer to others because she was "needed." Being a nice people-pleaser also made her feel good. She believed the lie that everything was all right, and the pain was buried deeper. That person was me.

An emotional mess is the way I could best describe my life at that time, but I didn't know it. Those who know something about the Lord can attest that often it is that emptiness that will cause us to run to Him. We realize that no one else can totally pull us out of this state, and we long to be in the presence of the Lord, never leaving from the position of sitting at the Father's feet. Family, friends or other people may not be around at all, but not the Lord. He will embrace us, stay with us, and let us know with His gentle whisper that everything will be alright if we trust Him.

A Moment to Reflect:

Do you know someone (or read about someone) who seems to have it all together? If so, how does that make you feel?

_____

_____

_____

Do you feel you have to wear a mask at home, at work, at church or elsewhere? If so, why?

_____

_____

_____

Do you ever feel empty? If so, do you find yourself at the feet of the Father, or do you have another way of "getting it together?"

_____

_____

_____

CHAPTER 2
The Fictitious Life

I do not know too many people who would not describe some part of their childhood or current family situation as somewhat dysfunctional based on their definition of perfect. This is especially true in comparison to others we think are living the good life. The Merriam-Webster dictionary defines "dysfunctional" as "not functioning properly; marked by impaired or abnormal functioning." To say that we are perfect would mean we are without faults or defects. Some describe it as being precisely accurate or as good as it could possibly be. Do you know anyone who fits the perfect description? It could be "yes" for some; however, I suppose it would depend on how one defines perfect.

Even with my definition of the not-so-perfect things that went on in my own life, I still envisioned the perfect television family from decades ago. Some of you may be too young to remember them. Though some of the shows were recorded before I was born, the old classics found their way in my television show line-up because of their rich family values.

The vision of what I thought resembled the picture-perfect family included a white picket fence wrapped around the home. The rich green lawn was always freshly manicured. The husband and wife resolved their differences (if they had any) in perfect harmony. The couple included humor in their differences of opinions as they worked things out. Their well-behaved children stepped straight out of "the school of obedience" with very few problems. The inside of the house was the image of a staged home with everything in perfect order. The wife (and mother) was neatly groomed first thing in the morning as she prepared a hot breakfast for the family to enjoy at the table together, and packed lunches for each family member. Dinnertime was set aside for family conversation around the table over a hot, home-cooked meal. The neighbors all got along with one another, demonstrated community and that it truly took a village pulling together to make it work. Everyone looked out for not only their own, but for each other.

Seems unreal, right? Well, I thought this was the perfect picture of family life, and not so strangely, I saw myself that way. Was that too much to ask or hope for? It was the classic image of the Proverbs 31 woman. Why couldn't I be the one rising early, perfectly put together before my husband even thought about getting up? Why not be the one to have a hot breakfast prepared for my family, making sure everything was ready for my husband's departure for work, packing lunches and my children's needed items ready to go to school? After doing all the normal things, there would be plenty of time to get myself together to start tackling my daily to-do list, checking the boxes on everything. That was a nice picture, but certainly not the way my life turned out.

I married the man I loved at the time; however, our love was not enough to sustain the marriage. The marriage ended in divorce after attempts on both sides to try to make it work. I felt I had given up on or put some of my dreams on hold to be with him. I cannot say the entire marriage was a mistake because out of that union came a wonderful child.

After the separation I spent many nights crying. I was hurting so bad and thinking about how much I failed in the relationship. Should I have done something differently? Soon the feelings of unhappiness piled up. This went on for years, and somewhere during the process, the root of rejection reared its ugly head. My own feelings of low self-esteem and unworthiness surfaced as problems escalated. I turned to food as a source of comfort. I don't know whether I thought the mirror was lying or that a spirit of deception had taken over because I didn't believe what I was seeing in the mirror. Then I stopped looking.

As I went through my separation which eventually led to the divorce, I didn't realize that I had put on a mask to hide my feelings of hurt, rejection and shame. However, during this process I realized that the root of rejection did not start there; it started in the womb. My parents didn't treat me differently than they treated my siblings, but during my healing process I had to uncover and revisit some things to move forward.

Several songs became my theme as I built a fortified wall up around me. I filled my spirit with songs such as "No More Tears" by Anita Baker and "I Will Survive" by Gloria Gaynor. I would listen to them over and over until the words took root and I started to believe them. Don't get me wrong, I love both songs and they carry a lot of meaning even today; however, at that time in my life, playing them repeatedly built a stronghold in an already wounded heart. I didn't know that by not mixing a little sweet with my bitterness that I was building a high wall and a hard place around myself and my heart to keep others away from me. I had put myself in prison by the words of my mouth until the realization came. Then I wanted to be free and cried out. (By the way, I can happily say that today, if I hear those songs, it's just good music with a meaning.)

As years went by, I had to be the mother and the father to our child because of the miles between us and my ex-husband, not because he was not supportive. I became extremely busy with things in my life to forget about the hurt I was feeling. I became so good at the busyness that it worked, or at least I thought it did. Yes, I knew God but not in the way I needed to know Him. I failed to get to know Him as my healer and deliver.

A Moment to Reflect:

For the most part, how would you describe your home life growing up and why?

_____

_____

_____

Did you ever envision how your life would be when you became an adult? If so, did it turn out that way? Why or why not?

_____

_____

_____

Did you ever turn to an addictive behavior or substance (food, excessive spending, alcohol, drugs, or other) to cope?

_____

_____

_____

CHAPTER 3
Alone at Last

The real unveiling began when I realized that my life was empty. It was because I was dancing solo without experiencing the Father's love.

July 16, 2002 started off just like any other ordinary day; however, little did I know that it would have such an impact on me and my journey. I'm sure there had been a knock at the door of my heart before; I just didn't recognize it at the time as the start of my inner healing and rebuilding process. It was on this day that I realized that the Lord had been trying to put the pieces of my broken life back together, His way, not mine.

A co-worker blessed me with a little down time at a quiet bed and breakfast on the water. I thought I would use that time to prepare for a teaching I had to deliver at my church. I decided (notice I said, "I") that since this place was also close to Ocean City in Maryland, that I would drive there for an extra day of rest and relaxation. Little did I know that God had other plans for me on this retreat. What I thought was preparation for teaching turned out to be life changing, and it was only the beginning of an incredible dance.

As I was packing and gathering all the directions I needed (let me add, this was before electronic navigation systems), the strangest thing happened, or at least I thought it was strange at the time. I was able to pull everything I needed off the internet except the directions from the bed and breakfast to the nearby beach. Every time I tried to pull those directions, my computer would freeze and I would have to reboot. This was a slow, tedious process. I probably rebooted five times or more, rebuking every devil in my way each time before saying, "Oh, well, I'll get them at the bed and breakfast. Surely they can tell me how to get there because they are so close." But again, God had other plans that I was not aware of.

Early that morning on the day of my departure, I received Jeremiah 33:3:

> "Call to Me, and I will answer you, and show you great and mighty things, which you do not know."

I packed what I needed to prepare for the teaching I had to deliver upon return along with some extra reading materials from my shelf. I also packed attire for a day trip to the beach that I was planning (notice I said "I" again), along with a folding chair and sunscreen. Away I went.

As I was driving on the highway, I listened to a variety of Gospel music, especially songs on inner and emotional healing. I was thinking of all the other people who needed to hear those songs, and began calling their names out and praying for them. There was nothing wrong with praying for them; however, God began to speak to me as I repeatedly said, "Oh, I need to let this person and that person hear these songs." The Lord gently said, "No, My child. The person who needs to hear these songs is you." It was at that moment, on that highway (Route 50), with my dark shades on that the tears began to flow. Yes, it was I who was hurting. Now I'm not saying that the others were not, but the Lord wanted to deal with me and the wounds that I hadn't allowed to heal properly.

I arrived at the lovely bed and breakfast property on the Chesapeake Bay, checked in, changed my clothes, grabbed my bag of books, sunblock and my dark shades, and headed outside to sit before the beautiful body of water. I didn't want to dive directly into the teaching material, so I started with one of the extra books I brought with me for a little downtime reading material. Hidden by my dark shades the tears flowed as I turned each page because I saw myself on each one. Since it was a quiet bed and breakfast, no one saw me. Perhaps the Lord planned it this way. He was about to change and reorder some things in my life. He continued to speak to me by the water.

When I retired for the night, I found a praise music station on the radio and left it playing in my room. Around 1:00 a.m., I woke to a song with these words in the introduction: "Jesus, it's me, Your daughter. Can I talk to you?" It startled me. Was it real or my imagination? To this day, I still cannot locate the song nor do I know who the recording artist is. The words of that song ministered to me and once again, I was crying.

After I had joined the owner of the bed & breakfast and others who had arrived late the day before for a light breakfast, I headed back to my chair on the Chesapeake. I finished the book I had begun reading the day before and another smaller one on emotional healing; but I never prepared the teaching I needed for my church when I returned. I never got around to touching those materials, yet I knew that my life would never be the same. Because this was the Lord's doing, I also knew that He would prepare me with a ready word on that Sunday, just four days away.

This began my dance on emotional healing. I wanted to know what love is and I wanted the Lord to show me. I realized I needed deep inner healing. I was the one who needed to be made whole. I was the one who needed to be delivered from hurt. I was the one not walking in forgiveness by still holding things against those I thought had hurt me and owed me an apology. I was the one who did not have joy because I was still crying a lot of tears. I was the one still hiding behind a mask with no recognition that I was hurting. I was the one who still felt alone. I was the one still holding on to painful memories of my past. I was carrying excess baggage and it was weighing me down. I was wounded with a broken heart and the mask was a hiding place for a false personality.

It was then that I was reminded of the moment seven years prior when a co-worker wrote Psalm 6 on a piece of paper and handed it to me as I passed by her workspace. Verses six and seven grabbed my attention.

> "I am weary with my groaning; all night I make my bed swim; I drench my couch with my tears. My eye wastes away because of grief; it grows old because of all my enemies."

David (the writer of the psalm) shared some good news in verse nine.

> "The Lord has heard my supplication; the Lord will receive my prayer."

At that moment, I felt that the Lord heard my supplication (my personal cry), received my prayers and would begin the process to heal my wounds to break through the callouses of my broken heart. I had been looking for people to justify me. I had been looking for false love. I had been looking for love in all the wrong places while the Lord was there all the time. It was during this time that I realized I wanted to be free without a mask.

A Moment to Reflect:

Have you ever felt the Lord calling you to a private getaway? If so, did you go willingly?

_____

_____

_____

Have you had times when others around you tried to get your attention on a matter needing correction? If so, how did you respond?

_____

_____

_____

Have you ever had plans to go somewhere to do something specific and your plans were interrupted by God? If so, what did you learn from it?

_____

_____

_____

CHAPTER 4
I Want to Be Free

The Word of God tells us in John 8:32,

"*And you shall know the truth, and the truth shall make you free.*"

The question we should ask ourselves is: "Do I want to know the truth so that I can be free?" Knowing the truth may require us to uncover some things that we would rather leave covered. We may need to reopen some old wounds to get to the root of the problem. There is a process many businesses use when analyzing problems called "root-cause" analysis. This is applicable for healing our spirit, soul and body as well. At the leading of the Holy Spirit, we may need to revisit some people or places that caused pain. Remember, it's all with His leading.

When I was a little girl, if I fell and returned home crying, my mother would calm me down by hugging me and immediately taking care of my "boo-boo." Although I knew that when she finished doing what she needed to do, I would feel so much better, I never wanted her to really touch it because cleaning my open sore was painful. After all, I had a scrape from the injury which took off some of my skin and there was blood!

None of that ever bothered my mother. Not even my tears because she knew it had to be taken care of. She would get a washcloth, go to the medicine cabinet and grab the "boo-boo" supplies. She would wash off any dirt and blood, apply an antiseptic, and then dress it with that "red stuff" and a swab. I hated it because of the slight sting from that "red stuff" when it touched by boo-boo. Finally, my mom would cover it with a Band-Aid. My tears would dry up and I was ready to play again, as if nothing had happened.

But it didn't end there. I was fine as long as the scrape was covered because the covering was a protection. There were some days she would replace the Band-Aid with a fresh one to keep the wound covered. Life was good. The "boo-boo" was covered, but according to my mom, it could not stay covered. I knew the day would come when my mom would say, "It's time to take the Band-Aid off." This was necessary so the scab could form and eventually fall off.

I would respond with a resounding, "No!" The traumatic memory would emerge of times I had fallen on the same spot after the Band-Aid was removed and caused the wound to open again. But my mom was never moved by those tears, and I knew better than to have a fit. Gently, she would remove the Band-Aid and comfort me by letting me know, it was good for the "boo-boo."

In my little "boo-boo" incidents, an application of dressing worked because it was only a scrape. However, there are many wounds today that are not due to a little scrape on the surface. They are deeply embedded wounds in our hearts that cannot be dressed up and covered with a little "red stuff" and a Band-Aid. That is a temporary fix which will not last. The only way complete healing can happen is if the root of the problem is uncovered to reveal the root-cause (the truth behind the cover-up), and by addressing the situation. But many choose to stay covered with Band-Aids because they are not willing to go through this process because it's painful. It's more painful than a little washcloth and the sting from the "red stuff". That sting lasting a brief moment is one thing; however, to deal with ugliness hiding behind something is another. Needless to say, if we don't uncover the wounds, others will see us walking around covered in Band-Aids looking like a patched-up mess.

The question is, are we only interested in dressing the wounds to cover them or addressing the wounds to open them up for healing? Our answer will depend on whether we want a temporary fix or permanent freedom. Freedom is a release from something an individual is holding onto or hiding in an unhealthy way. Once we are released, something new will happen.

> "Then Jesus said to those Jews who believed Him, 'If you abide in My word, you are My disciples indeed. And you shall know the truth, and the truth shall make you free.' They answered Him, 'We are Abraham's descendants, and have never been in bondage to anyone. How can You say, "You will be made free"?' Jesus answered them, 'Most assuredly, I say to you, whoever commits sin is a slave of sin. And a slave does not abide in the house forever, but a son abides forever. Therefore if the Son makes you free, you shall be free indeed.'"
> (John 8:31-37)

The kind of freedom described in that passage is a new kind of release. Once we accept Jesus Christ as our Lord and Savior and begin to understand the truth in His word, something happens, we change. Old mindsets are broken off. Old ways of thinking are torn down. Our old identity is gone. We have a new identity along with a rich inheritance.

This kind of release produces a new vision of life. It's a new release from the past. It's a new release from condemnation, guilt and shame. It's a new release from old ways of thinking. It's a release from captivity. It's a release that won't cost you anything except a relationship with Jesus Christ and a heart that's willing to change. When the new person emerges after the change through acceptance of Jesus Christ as their personal Savior to start this process, or for those already in a relationship with Jesus, a release from a place of bondage, we now become available to do the work God created us to do. Others will see this new release.

In the book of Exodus, we read about an enslaved group of people, the Israelites, who spent a lot of time in the wilderness after their miraculous escape, mainly due to their own disobedience. However, we should not be so quick to judge others' enslavement or disobedience that could keep them stuck in certain cycles. We, too, can be enslaved either through situations we had no control over or ones that were self-inflicted. Bondage is slavery and deliverance is freedom. Just because we find ourselves entangled in bondage does not mean that we need to stay that way. If we cry out to the Lord, He will hear us and help us. We may not agree with the method He chooses as our way out; however, His way will always be the best way. It's while walking with the Lord that we learn to trust at a deeper level and our faith increases.

There are many forms of slavery that keep us in bondage. Some of them include, but are not limited to:

> Slavery to finances due to personal bad financial decisions rather than loss of income beyond our control.
>
> Slavery to addictions in all forms, such as overeating, sexual sins, drugs, alcohol, and many more that come with negative effects.
>
> Slavery to overworking that leads to stress and potential health problems.
>
> Slavery to unhealthy relationships leading to unhealthy soul ties.
>
> Slavery to unforgiveness which can lead to all kinds of illnesses and loss of peace of mind.
>
> Slavery to generational sins, repeating unhealthy patterns of iniquity from our ancestral line. It's important to know history to have understanding.

During my own personal journey with the Lord, several biblical examples were explored; however, there was a common denominator as a key to help. There was a cry out that led to deliverance. In other words, the one crying out wanted to be free. I'm totally convinced that if we cry out to God for help, just as He did for others, He will also help us. God will hear us from His holy hill (Psalm 3:4). The key is to cooperate with God by trusting His method so that we can be delivered in less time than the forty years it took to deliver the Israelites! It boils down to uncovering the hidden things and our obedience.

A Moment to Reflect:

Do you have a Band-Aid on you now that you want to take off? If so, how hard is it to take off and why?

_____

_____

_____

Do you want to be set free from the problem(s)?

_____

_____

_____

Are you willing to cry out to God and trust Him for the answer and course of direction?

_____

_____

_____

CHAPTER 5
The Restoration Process

One day as I was going through some items in a room and remembered that I had purchased a can of wood finish to restore a piece of furniture that had been passed down through the generations. Since the furniture was in a space not frequently used, I had forgotten all about that project.

A family member was visiting with me at the time and volunteered to take on that project, insisting that she was skilled to do it. She informed me of other items needed in order to start and finish the project which was more than my small can of wood finish. Items included protection for the floor, sandpaper, a brush and a finishing gloss. After listening to the list, I was reminded of why I had put the project aside. I needed more than the can of finisher in addition to time to complete the project; therefore, it went on my ever-growing to-do list.

When I looked at the furniture, I noticed a testing area where I tried to take a shortcut by just laying on a coat of the finisher without sanding it first and it didn't turn out so good. In other words, no shortcuts are allowed when doing this type of project especially if you want it to look good. My father used to say, "If you're not going to do something right, then don't do it at all." I took that advice on this project.

Oh, the joy of the restoration process! Just think about the scraping away (or the sanding) with sandpaper to remove the old. If you've ever felt sandpaper against your skin or heard it being scraped against something, it sounds painful. Careful attention is given to restore the item to its natural beauty by applying the new coat making it look new. Finally, the glossy sealing coat is added for protection and to bring out the shine, producing a beautiful piece of furniture.

That's the process of restoration in the natural. It's not a quick fix, it's a process. Some people find this entire process therapeutic. Restoration takes time. Those who enjoy this take the time to do it. We take time to restore furniture like this to make it usable again. God takes even more care to restore us.

God takes the time to pull out what's been pushed into a back room behind a closed door. Often, it's in a closed, unused, dark space. He takes the time to make sure everyone and everything needed is available to do the work. He takes the time to gently get rid of the old to put on the new. He takes the time to restore the beauty in us that He originally created us to have. God is not concerned about how long it takes when we are willing because He says we're worth it. We just need a heart that says, "Yes, Lord" and be willing to follow Him. Although the price was paid on the cross by Jesus, His Son, it will cost us complete surrender to let Him lead the dance His way.

A Moment to Reflect:

Name at least one area in your life that you feel needs to be restored.

_____

_____

_____

Have you ever asked God to restore that area in your life? Why or why not?

_____

_____

_____

Knowing that restoration is a process, are you now willing to go through the process, which may include a little sandpaper? Why or why not?

_____

_____

_____

CHAPTER 6
The Soul Closet

The Lord shined light on my busyness. It was all the things I had added to my plate to avoid dealing with the buried hurt that I didn't want to face. There were doors I needed to close from my past so I could unlock the doors to my future. I also realized I had to reopen some doors I had previously closed to see what was in there, and to clean them out so I could close them for good. It was time for some internal spring cleaning, and time to clean out the closet to my soul.

I had to open many personal closets I didn't want to open to begin cleaning out the clutter that had accumulated in my heart for many years. I had to turn the lights on in those dark places and go through things bit by bit, slat by slat, and item by item. Because this had not been revisited on a frequent basis as a bi-annual closet cleaning, issues had piled up to the point of being buried so deep that I had to go in. I often asked myself during the process, "How did I get like this?" Later I realized that it wasn't so much how I got there, but that I had to clean it up and do what was needed to move forward.

Have you ever been forced to clean or fix something because it was broken? I have. Or perhaps something needed a little straightening up or fixing but it wasn't urgent on the list of things to do until it started to bother you. Either way, the job had to be done by somebody.

When I was growing up, we did annual spring cleaning. In fact, it seemed that the entire neighborhood participated at the same time with both external and internal cleaning. Every year, right around the beginning of spring, neighbors would open their windows (of course we didn't have all the allergies then) and everyone could smell the aroma of pine, lemon and other fresh-smelling cleaning products being used to welcome in spring. Every slat on window blinds were washed and walls in every room were wiped down to get rid of the winter soot from the furnaces. Furniture was dusted, hardwood floors were waxed, and laundry was washed and hung outside to dry in the sun. Lawns were nicely manicured and flower beds were planted. All of this and so much more were associated with spring cleaning. Then bi-annually, we would clean out our closets. Time was spent to get rid of any clutter that had been stacked away, and to give away all the clothes and shoes that we had outgrown from the previous seasons. This analogy is big spiritually for our souls too.

In the house I grew up in we never had a problem with a closet rack falling because it was a sturdy rod. No matter how many clothes were stuffed in there (and as siblings we shared a closet), the rod they hung on never fell.

I think most of us can attest to the fact that some things are just not made the way they use to be, and closets are one of them. Growing up we had those strong closet rods that were partly in the wall on each end and bolted in. The closets were smaller (many not walk-in), and one could hang several garments on that one rod and stuff many other clothing items in between and it just remained in place. There were no fancy shelves attached, no wire racks, no storage for shoes, or any other compartments, just a solid, strong rod. However, I can truly say that it has not been the case in most modern dwelling places today with wire racks as the standard without any upgrades. I can't tell you how many times I have hung up a piece of clothing and either immediately or sometime afterwards heard a thump and found the entire rack and all my clothing on the floor.

With modern apartments and houses today, over the years, I've had several closet rods collapse on me. Yes, there were a lot of clothes hanging in them, but no more than a sturdy rod had once held. Most times when this happened, I really didn't have time to deal with it. All

I could think about was emptying everything from the closet one more time so I could have someone come in to fix it again. I dreaded the very thought of it.

Not only would everything be on the floor, the anchorage holding the racks in place would be ripped out of the wall. Before it could be repaired, the clothes had to be removed from the fallen wire rack along with anything that could get in the way of the wall repair job. It was always a big task for me because of the amount of clothes. This has happened more than once in my lifetime. It's one of those things that when it happens, you just let out a disgusted sigh because you know what needs to be done, and there is no more room on your full to-do list to deal with a closet. So, as with anything I don't want to do, I would procrastinate. I would leave the closet in a fallen state for quite some time and work around it.

Finally, one day, probably when I was frustrated looking for something, I heard, "You can't just keep looking at it and not deal with it. After all, it always looks worse before it looks better." Now that spontaneous thought did not come from me because I was happy with my frustrated work-around and perfectly fine with not fixing it at that moment. I was in no rush because of the work involved with pulling everything out of the closet. But God had another plan and another lesson in life for me to learn.

Sometimes, we have things buried deep in the closets of our mind and heart, hidden so deep within that we would rather not deal with them. As a matter of fact, as long as we keep the doors closed, no one will ever know while we continue to work around the mess. But God knows. I'm convinced that God wants to partner with us to clean the clutter of our collapsed mind and heart to build us back up, sturdier and stronger than ever before. But it will be "all Him and none of us." With God as our Master Builder, we will be built with endurance to last.

When I realized that I wanted to be free, I was bound with no room to work around in my fallen, cluttered closet. It was time to bring in the Master Builder.

A Moment to Reflect:

Was there ever a time that the Lord shined light on clutter in your heart? If so, name one?

_____

_____

_____

Did you leave it in a fallen, clutter state for a while? Why or why not?

_____

_____

_____

How do you feel about the situation now?

_____

_____

_____

CHAPTER 7

The Beasts in the Basement

Now that the closet was done, it seemed that the real work was just about to begin. It would mean going deeper to get to the root structure that was causing so many limbs to sprout, each one entwining and entangling with another. If you've ever studied or looked at the root structure of a tree you would see that. Little by little, we must get rid of them to rid ourselves of the entanglements and get free. The Word of God says in John 8:32 that we shall know the truth and the truth shall set us free.

Just as the annual spring cleaning and closet fixing was a big ordeal for me, the basement was another. I refer to this period in my life as my personal spring cleaning to deal with the "beasts" in the basement.

I'm not sure if my family ever knew this but I had a real fear of basements growing up. Now let me define what a basement was like for me. There are homes today that have basements where you can walk out through a sliding glass door or some type of door into the backyard. I'm not talking about that. I'm talking about a real basement that is truly underground with a full set of steps to exit out and with windows equal to the ground level outside. That is a basement. It is a place where you are truly underground along with other things that belong underground including the root structure of trees.

The first house where I spent most of my years growing up was a two-bedroom house with one of those basements. The basement was the place where we did laundry and where the furnace was located. At one time it was fixed up as our bedroom to give us more space as children while freeing up an extra bedroom upstairs for guests. As a matter of fact, most children were thrilled to move to the basement because it felt like their space.

Although it was normal for people in the neighborhood to fix up the basement and utilize it as an extra room, I never really liked being in the basement. No matter how much bright paint was used, it still felt dark to me. No matter how sealed it was, it was still underground where other things live or once lived before the foundation had been laid. It represented dreariness to me. It represented the "stuff underneath."

The light was up in the ceiling. To pull the switch to turn it on and off, my father added a cord we could easily reach. My other family members would pull the cord and then come up the steps but not me. I would walk as far up the steps as I could, reach over the rail (it was safe), pull the cord and then run up the steps as fast as my short legs could carry me, quickly closing the door behind me. All I knew was that once the light was out it was dark. I could be down there most of the day but for some reason, I thought that once the light was out while I was walking up the steps, someone or something would grab my legs between the slats on the railing leading upstairs.

In my book, *Make This House Into A Home* (Portman, 2015), I describe a similar revelation after having watched the movie, *Are We Done Yet?* (Hartley et al. & Carr, 2007). In summary, a family was looking for a larger house and found the home of their dreams. It was away from the noise of the city, the landscaping was beautiful, the neighbors were friendly (like the "welcome wagon" everyday), the inside was gorgeous, the office was perfect for the aspiring magazine writer, and the price was right. The realtor really promoted the house on their walk-through noting a few "minor repairs" that were needed. The family purchased the home, and after they moved in things started to go wrong in the house. They had not been noticeable during the walk-through because they were below the surface. Every time something else was uncovered that needed repairing, a crew was brought in to fix it. The house was a total mess due to all the major renovations to repair all the things below the surface.

The main point was the house had a lot of value but needed some work. Likewise, we are valuable to God, and He knows what is hiding underneath the surface. Our outside appearance can say one thing, but it's the stuff in our soul that screams about something more that we need to deal with to allow the Holy Spirit to fully occupy us.

This reminds me of what happens to us after we accept Jesus as our personal Savior. We become new creatures and the Holy Spirit moves into our house. A spiritual transformation happens. Things that are below the surface can resurface, and we must deal with them. But this transformation is not to torment us. It's to bring us into the fulfillment of the things God wants to do in our lives.

It's almost like preparing for a move but intentional. If you've ever been involved in moving, it can be quite an ordeal. We often find boxes we have not opened in a long time, tucked away in some extra room, basement or garage. Since they are hiding in rooms that we don't typically use, they are out of sight, out of mind. Because we are rushed to vacate one place to get to the next, instead of going through them before we move, sometimes we load them up and transport the unopened boxes to our new home. These boxes represent things we have not gone through or dealt with and often, it is years of accumulation.

Now all these boxes of "stuff" are in our new place. Some may contain painful memories packed and tucked away in yet another room. Once again, we think, "I'll go through them one day when I have time but for now, I'll leave them here in the basement, attic, garage or room." And for many of us, that one day never comes. Once again, they are out of sight, out of mind, and we sort of hope they will go away. We know we haven't touched them in all these years, and we probably don't need the contents inside; but just in case there is one thing in there we need, we had better go through them to be sure. I'm not recommending to just toss them, but there should be time set aside to go through them.

This is true when it comes to our inner healing. We pack stuff in the basement of our heart and take them from place to place, dragging them along as God is trying to heal us. In the new place of healing, we have brought the boxes and stored them in a dark, hidden place. Unless a door is opened and the switch is turned on, they remain in that closed space until the next time we must go there to deal with the packed boxes.

Not all of it is individual. Sometimes we see repeated cycles of undealt-with boxes in our family. We must go underneath the surface, back in history to understand the "why" behind it. Once we begin to research certain actions in our family history, our eyes are opened to see the situation clearer, answering many questions. God values family relationships and longs to heal them, but we must be willing to deal with the stuff tucked away. As with any major cleaning task, it always looks worse when we start pulling everything out; however, once we complete the task, it's a beautiful thing. God sees value in us even through all the work that needs to be done.

During my basement experience, things were uncovered. Rejection reared its ugly head and I had to deal with all the roots that were wrapped around it causing entanglement. Shame surfaced on all fronts and I had to deal with that, too. Some real ugly truths came out, but after all, I asked to be free, right? So, the process continued at a deeper level.

A Moment to Reflect:

Do you recognize some things tucked away in a hidden space in your heart that is out of sight, out of mind? If so, name at least one.

_____

_____

_____

Are there family matters that could be tucked away in a hidden space that really should be dealt with? If so, name at least one.

_____

_____

_____

Do you have a desire to turn the light on and open the box? If not, what is holding you back?

_____

_____

_____

CHAPTER 8
Push Past the Pain

After the Lord showed me where rejection entered in my life, I was able to see how my self-esteem had been damaged. Then He took me through a process of reading the Song of Solomon in the Bible. The first time I read it, I saw it as a love relationship between me and God. When I read it a second time, I saw a love relationship with myself. Finally, during my third time reading it through, I saw a love relationship between a man and woman.

Because I was battling low self-esteem, rejection and shame, the Lord showed me a personal model to use for my own learning about love. First, see the Lord as my lover, then love myself, and then I'll be able to see and receive love from others. So often, we try to do the reverse. We enter into relationships with others before having one with God and ourselves. It's hard to give love to someone else without an understanding of what true love is. I found myself saying to the Lord, "I want to know what love is and I want You to show me," and He answered. I had to continue the workout of my soul in the area of love, trust and acceptance, all additional steps towards helping me become whole.

Our bodies need some type of physical activity for health and wellness. In the same way, we need to exercise our spiritual soul with greater intensity. When I began a workout regimen a few years ago, I had the opportunity to glean from the advice of a few professional trainers. Although there was a lot of common knowledge between them, I noticed that each trainer had their own set of instructions about stretching, working out and eating.

Some would tell me to stretch before the workout; some would tell me to stretch after the workout. Some would tell me to eat mini meals throughout the day on a timed scheduled; while others did not put an emphasis on how many meals per day to eat, but rather to watch the types of foods I ate. Even with the differences in information, the one common thread was that to meet my weight loss goals and see results, I had to push myself beyond my own comfort level. When I would hit a plateau without reaching my goal, I had to do something different to push past it. One thing was evident: without having a little bit of pain, there would be no gain.

I took a water aerobics class a few times and really enjoyed it. It felt great because the buoyancy of the water assisted with the workout. I never really noticed the full benefits while in the water because it was refreshing and fun. It wasn't until I climbed the stairs to get out of the pool that I realized the workout I thought wasn't doing too much was really doing everything. I worked muscles that I forgot I had, and I felt them.

The soul workout is like a physical workout except it's with our soul. We exercise our spiritual muscles so they can be developed and strengthened. We may not start the process with joy; however, when we finish, we feel great and look great. To have the type of workout that brings healing to our soul and produces lasting results, we must be willing to push ourselves beyond our comfort level to deal with the deeply rooted, internal issues that had built up plaque in our hearts, causing a hardening that only God can remove. Removing the layers of plaque can be painful, but it's a good pain.

During my process of inner healing, I cannot recall how many prayer conferences, retreats or women's conferences I attended where someone prayed personal prayers of healing and deliverance over me. Whether I hit the floor (out in the Spirit) or was still standing, the thought was the same, "Why am I getting that same word? I thought that was gone from the last conference." Finally, enough was enough. I decided to make an appointment with one of my pastors at that time to gain a better understanding. Not only was she a pastor, but she also had a degree in counseling.

She explained that we might have twenty layers of hurt on us. Someone prays for us and maybe ten layers come off, leaving the other ten to deal with. Then something happens that sparks five of those ten that came off to come back on, and now instead of ten, you have fifteen, but it's still not the twenty you started with. With this newfound knowledge, I really wanted to be free of anything that was holding me back, so I determined to work hard to get there.

I fasted and prayed because I wanted the Lord to show me anything that was still holding me back. Alone in my home, I found myself laying on the floor and once again, crying out Him to heal me. As I was praying, I saw a sharp object that resembled a long knife or sword sticking through me. I began to hear certain things to break off me spiritually, including some generational issues, so I did it. I got up feeling pretty good, standing in my kitchen praying to the Lord, happy that was over. That was until I went to church that evening and ended up in another prayer line.

It was my pastor at the time who prayed over me. He ended by saying, "And I see the big sword sticking in your stomach," and he made a motion, a spiritual enactment to pull it out. He ended the prayer asking the Lord to heal me. I thought, "What was that about? I already saw that object and thought I prayed over it." When I returned home, I inquired of the Lord and He answered, "Yes, I showed you the sword sticking in you, but you never took it out."

I finally got it. Inner healing would be a process and if I wanted true freedom, it would be up to me to continue the journey in full cooperation with the Lord. And the best news is that He will help us.

Another area I faced was trust. While lifting weights at a gym, a friend began to walk me through various machines, explaining proper technique so I wouldn't hurt myself with the weights. I went to the bench press and was using my normal amount of weights with my normal amount of reps when he decided to increase them slightly. As he was piling on the additional weights, I told him they would be too heavy; however, he insisted I add the weights and said, "I got you." My thought was, "But you're not the one doing the lifting." He paid no attention to me as he added the additional poundage.

I began the reps and he stood there watching every lift, counting and encouraging me, not giving me a chance to express how fatigued my muscles were getting. Then something changed. I noticed that after I had completed a couple of sets, my pace got slower as I began to struggle just a little. He put his hand on the middle of the bar. I wanted to quit, so I said, "You're going to let this drop on me." But he kept encouraging me with his hand still on the bar saying, "I got you, keep going. I'm not going to let it drop."

Suddenly, I trusted him because the weights began to feel lighter. He encouraged me as I pumped the bar up and down. I watched his hand go up and down in sync with mine on the bar. It occurred to me that he was really the one doing most of the lifting now, taking on all the weight, making it easy for me. Then the thought came that God does that with us. We are never the ones carrying, pushing or pumping the weight, He is. Just when we think we've given it our last push, suddenly, what we thought we were carrying feels weightless.

When I mentioned this to my son, the light bulb completely came on. Being one who lifts weights, he explained that the job of a spotter is very important, that's why they workout in pairs. The spotter is to always be alert and positioned properly to assist especially if they notice that the person is beginning to struggle. When that happens, they are to either lessen the weight with their assistance or totally remove it. But here's the key. He ended by saying, "And, a spotter is to never take his or her eyes off of you." What a revelation! If that is the role of a natural spotter, just image what our Heavenly Father provides to us. He knows how to watch over us. He promised to never put more on us than what we can bear. He promised to never leave us. Wow! God is our spotter!

There were various things the Lord took me through to push past the pain so that I could love, be loved and trust again. In some cases, I had to be reminded of the point of entry to deal with it, which was painful. There were many people I had to forgive, and things I had to let go. Now I can answer the question others ask me, "How do you know that you've let something go?" My response is that when it's brought up, the same bitter emotions won't stir you. We may not forget what others have done to us or some of our own self-inflicted wounds; however, our response will be much different. The negative emotions won't be there.

A Moment to Reflect:

Is there a passage in the Bible that you remember as one that really spoke to your identity during a painful moment? What is the passage?

_____

_____

_____

What do you remember as some of the lessons the Lord was trying to teach you during this time?

_____

_____

_____

Was the process painful, yet with much gain? Describe it.

_____

_____

_____

CHAPTER 9
Truth Hurts, But It Heals

Facing the truth can be hard at times. When we are around others or conversing with them, it's easy to see their weaknesses and sometimes, we find ourselves offering them advice on what they need to do to change their circumstances. However, isn't it strange that when we look in the mirror at ourselves, we can look at the same image every day without seeing our true reflection?

In 1987, Michael Jackson recorded a song entitled, "Man in the Mirror." What I received from the song was that each one of us must look at ourselves to see what we must change about ourselves to help make the world a better place. If you take a moment to listen to the lyrics quietly, you can pick up several nuggets that set the stage for dealing with the truth about ourselves. Instead of looking at everyone else as a source of the problems around us, every individual should look at themselves to see how they can make a positive difference. With that, I started looking at myself in the mirror, the mirror to my hurting soul. I cried out to God more than once, and He answered me. I wanted to look in the mirror and see more of the Lord and less of me. I wanted my character to reflect the One I called my God, my Father.

This works hand-in-hand with acknowledging the problem to get to freedom. It's taking a good look in the mirror of our soul, acknowledging the problem, crying out for help, accepting and trusting the help God sends along the way as His plan for freedom, and making up our mind to never go back to the place of bondage again. That's what God took the Israelites through in the book of Exodus in the Bible, and we have the same promise of help through His Son, Jesus Christ.

In addition to looking at ourselves, it is also hard to hear the truth from a friend or someone else. It is one thing to say we want people who can be a real friend and be honest with us, it's another to receive what they say from a place of love. Sometimes we are the only ones in the room without a sense of smell and unable to smell our own mess.

If you've ever had children or have been around them, it won't take you long to imagine this scenario. As you read it, picture it. But first let me start by saying, children learned that "No" was a complete sentence a long time ago, and it is. No other explanation is needed when it's used. They know that the word means don't do something, I'm not going to do something, or I'm not going to come to you. Depending on the situation, we may find ourselves turning our heads to laugh before bringing the necessary parental or guardian correction.

I was chatting with the Lord about this, just having a general conversation about a lot of stuff and asking questions. Then suddenly, because I'm a visual person, He showed me an image of a little baby running around with a very full diaper. Now here is where you must use your imagination so you can see what I saw. It was quite comical but true.

Have you ever seen a baby running around with a diaper so full that it's puffy in the front and back, not to mention smelly? It's also so full and puffy that their walk even changes to one that's slew-footed. I think they know something is wrong but don't want to stop doing what they're doing long enough to get changed; therefore, they go on about their way.

When we notice it, we say something like, "Come here. Let me change your diaper." They very boldly and proudly say, "No," and continue doing what they were involved in, and we go after them. They run very slew-footed, laughing (or not) all the way. Eventually, we catch up to them and diverting their attention (or not) we manage to get the diaper changed.

As God was showing me this, He said, "That's how it is with My children. Oftentimes they are running around so full of their own mess but won't stop long enough to allow Me to change them." Imagine the laughter that roared out of me. Oh, how true that is. Sometimes we are so full of our own mess but won't allow (or want) Him to change us. We run around, puffy and slew-footed until we decide to get changed. It is not a swagger that we have, it's a walk full of stuff that everyone else can see (and smell) except us.

Change happens when we take a deep, honest look at situations and decide to make positive changes. Change happens when we can admit that we need to change and seek the proper help. Making a change to become better is a positive thing. One of the best things is that change can be contagious. When we change for the best, it will rub off on others. Said another way, when we change for the Best (God), He will rub off on others.

This kind of change is better than any scrubbing bubbles. It's better than any Roto-Rooter system. It's better than any natural cleansing systems we purchase in health stores. It's better than any gunk remover products we use in cars or sinks. The best news of all is, He is our guide. If you're a Christian, you understand that the Holy Spirit lives inside of us because we have accepted Jesus as our Lord and Savior. He is the Word and with the living Word inside of us, He gets the junk out by transforming us through renewing our mind.

God is not concerned about how many degrees or titles we have before or after our name. He's concerned about our emotional well-being. He's concerned about us living out our purpose while here on earth to make a positive difference somewhere. He's concerned about how we represent Him on a daily basis.

A Moment to Reflect:

Read the passage of 2 Samuel 12:1-14, the story of Nathan the prophet going to David the king to let him know of his (David's) sin. Is there a person in your life like Nathan? How do you receive them?

_____

_____

_____

Read the passage in John 4:1-29, the story of the Samaritan woman at the well who had an encounter with Jesus. Think about a time when someone shared something personal about your situation that was the truth. What was your response?

_____

_____

_____

Read the passage in Matthew 23:1-30 where Jesus addressed the Scribes and Pharisees. Is there a moment in your life when you were either the receiver of a hard word of truth or when you had to deliver a similar one? Describe it.

_____

_____

_____

CHAPTER 10

A Blessing in the Wilderness

There are many things we get excited about; however, I don't think being routed through the wilderness is one of them. Think about the wilderness for a moment. It is defined as "a barren desert or uncultivated region, suitable for pasturage and occupied by nomads. It's a dry, river-less and barren place."[1] In other words, it's a very lonely place, yet God sometimes will choose this route for us to strengthen us and free us from life's bondages. This sounds strange for someone wanting to deliver His people from bondage, right? However, since God knows what is best for us and what we need to be equipped and prepared for at our next place, we are led in.

God knows what we can handle during certain seasons. Isn't it good to know that if He called us out of a situation and leads us on a particular route, there must be a reason for it? While the Israelites were in the wilderness God took care of them by providing sweetened water for them, refreshing them by the twelve springs of water and seventy palm trees, supplying manna for them daily and providing water from a rock. He provided protection. He answered Moses's intercessory prayer and provided the support of Aaron and Hur (while Joshua led Israel in a victorious battle); and appointed seventy elders to serve under him (Exodus 15-18).

---

1   Zondervan's Understand the Bible Reference Series. <u>New International Bible Dictionary</u>. 1987, pp. 1064-1065.

Disobedience can cause us to wander a little longer in the wilderness than God intended. His chosen way to deliver us may not be the shortest route. It could be that the shortest way is not the best route because it may be in the detours (or wilderness) that our trust relationship develops as we follow Him. In Exodus 13:17-18, it states that God led them by way of the wilderness so they would not change their minds. Surely if God led the Israelites through the wilderness, He would take care of them. Isn't that what Jesus did when He led the disciples to the other side of the sea in Mark 4:35-41 as the winds and waves beat the boat? (There is more on that in Chapter 15.) God is not trying to punish us in the process. He is trying to make us stronger in faith so when other challenges come before us, we will know that the same God who delivered us once will deliver us again when we cry out to Him.

Think about it in terms of taking a trip. In many cases taking the interstate highway may be the fastest way, especially if we are traveling between several states. We can travel at a higher rate of speed, have access to more lanes to maneuver around the slower travelers, have surety of more places to stop for breaks, and get there faster though with a little less scenery. However, God may send us by way of the scenic route where the speed limit is slower, where there are fewer places to stop, and where there is no passing lane to get around the slower traffic. We may feel as if it's taking forever to get to the next place. But, along this scenic route, there are other little "stopovers" where we pick up blessings, learn life lessons, meet different people needed for our destiny journey, and see the hand of God in it all the way.

There are times on this journey that taking the road less traveled can lead to something beautiful and answer many questions we had along the way. I had an opportunity to travel back country roads with a relative. If you've never experienced that before, let me set the stage for you. The country roads I'm talking about all looked the same with no street signs, and on many of them no markings were in sight. The locals refer to many of those roads as just that, "the road." They might name someone who lives on that road or a store as a landmark. Depending on how deep in the country you are, most roads will not have a street sign, it's a "road".

We started our journey passing by a surplus of fields, pine trees, and forests. They all looked the same to me; however, she knew exactly where to turn. She was my own personal, live navigation system. That was important because on these "roads", you just might lose mobile services.

After traveling down a few open roads, she would say something such as, "When you get around this corner, turn right (or left). Don't go too fast because you will miss the road." No street name was mentioned, just "the road." I didn't get lost with this relative in the car because she was a local. She kept directing me to turn right, turn left, follow this road, and on and on, while still carrying on a conversation when we were on an open stretch of "road".

As we traveled, I looked around for some landmarks to remember, but everything looked the same. She continued to tell me where to turn. Finally, we reached a "road" that looked like a path. It was not paved but it was accessible to automobiles and she told me to turn. Pine trees lined both sides of this "road." The car was rocking and rolling down the dirt path of this "road." It was certainly uneven, and all the while I thought, "I'm glad it's not raining because this would be a muddy mess!" But we were going somewhere.

I kept driving under her direction, bouncing and bobbing in the car. I could not see the end for the trees. As I was concentrating on the bumps in the road, she wasn't concerned about a thing. Finally, after one last rock and roll in the car, light broke through the trees and I knew something was ahead. At last, we reached our destination. The trees still lined both sides, grass and dirt still "paved" this "road;" however, it ended at a spot where I needed to capture a picture-perfect moment of my family history. It was a place where my great grandfather ran a ferry.

Traveling this road made me think about our spiritual journey. Sometimes it looks like the road less traveled for us because we chose to follow Jesus. There are no street signs, He just says, "Follow Me". We decided to go in a direction that's different from the majority because God said to go. We decided to stand on a decision because God said to stand. We decided to walk away from some people or things because God said to walk away. And it goes on and on.

The entire time we're doing this, we might be thinking, "I know God is telling me to go right, go left, go straight, but I sure can't see anything through this forest of trees." We might even look back and discover that nobody else is following us; however, we're following God's voice and His footsteps on the "road". We're on a journey with our Father. Then suddenly, we get past the blanket of tall pines, we manage to survive the rocking and rolling through the bumps, and there is a breaking of day.

The journey we were on with God now makes perfect sense. We're smiling and grateful to be at the end of that "road," probably only to start a new journey on another "road". But now we can look back and say, "I took the road less traveled with God. Though it looked as if it was leading nowhere, it was really leading to somewhere, and I'm glad God never left me. Rather, He led me all the way through the rocks and bumps, and I made it."

I'm sure we've traveled many strange roads trusting our personal navigation systems to get us there. There may be times we don't know where we're going, yet we trust them to get us there. The route can be recalculated based on a wrong turn or traffic jam, and we continue to follow the route, trusting the system to get us to our destination.

If we place that much confidence in a computerized device, just think how much greater it would be to have the same confidence in God. After all, He knows our final destination, and all we have to do is jump in and enjoy the ride. There is nothing wrong with technology. It can be a wonderful thing; however, I once heard the Lord tell me, "I'm your personal navigation system, your GPS, and I can get you anywhere I need to take you through My word!"

> *"Your word is a lamp to my feet and a light to my path."*
> (Psalm 119:105)

The Holy Spirit is our personal navigation system, and step by step He guides us to the next place. Once we start our journey with God and allow Him to lead (and of course we must follow), we won't have any wrong turns, dead ends, bad locations, toll roads, or any other nuisances. The Holy Spirit will guide. His Word will be our directions and will lead us to the right place. Another good thing is that we won't lose heart even if we made a wrong turn because God certainly knows how to recalculate our route. We can enjoy "God's Personal System."

I can only imagine what anyone would think if they are told they're going to be led into the wilderness to get to their next location or place in life. Life in the wilderness cannot be imagined as a pleasant experience and once there, they realize that. Many questions arise and there is great anticipation of exiting. However, even in the midst of being there, lessons will be learned along the way.

During many of my own wilderness experiences, I felt abandoned. It seemed no one was around. Would anyone hear me if I cried out? There were times when I called someone just to have an ear and they didn't answer the phone. It was me and God. But it was during that time that I developed a deep dependency on Him and grew in my intimacy with God.

The wilderness is not a place where anyone would want to pitch a tent and camp forever. The times I was led into the wilderness, I looked for the fastest way out, but the nearest exit was nowhere to be found. Rather, I was told to "trust." Many tears were shed and there was much crying out. I was able to read the story of the Israelites journey in the wilderness with another set of eyes. My time alone with Him was invaluable.

During this time, God will pour more revelation into us. He will show us things we need to let go of to make the shifts. He will take us through some spiritual tests. He does a work in us by providing proper training. He does a work in other people we need along the journey to make sure they are properly positioned so connections can be made at the right time. He grows us spiritually in areas where we lack maturity.

He knows exactly what we need to make a successful transition because He would not set us up to fail.

Sometimes we end up in the wilderness due to our own disobedience; however, when God leads us into the wilderness, we are being equipped for our next assignment. It is the place we learn to rely on and trust God. It's the road less traveled, not the way we would choose to go. It means going in a direction that not too many people would want to travel with you. In fact, they might opt to take a plane and meet you there. It is a lonely road and a lonely walk; a place where your total dependence is on God the Father.

As we examine a portion of the life of Jesus in Luke 4, we find He went into the wilderness and passed every test while there. He came out and launched into ministry, performing miracles and dealing with difficult people and circumstances. If Jesus was led into the wilderness, do we really think we can escape that experience? Strength is gained in the wilderness. Wisdom is acquired in the wilderness. The wilderness has a place of entry and exit, and the exit is different from the way we entered.

You might have an entourage with you as long as you're running with the crowd; however, look behind you next time you're led into the wilderness and see how many have joined you on this route. And that may not be a bad thing because everyone cannot go where you're going. We will encounter enemies in the wilderness. We will face temptations in the wilderness. We may have to face a fear we need to overcome. Family and friends could reject us while we are in the wilderness. We could birth a business in the wilderness. We could be working on our own soul healing in the wilderness. It could be the time when God is at the potter's wheel doing His greatest work to shape and mold us (Jeremiah 18:1-4). The key is obedience so that more time is not spent there than what was intended.

A Moment to Reflect:

Are you or have you been on a path that seems to be the road less traveled? Describe it.

_____

_____

_____

What are some of your wilderness experiences? Were you led or did you end up there because of your own disobedience? If you have experienced both, what were some of the differences?

_____

_____

_____

Did you obey instructions while in the wilderness or do you feel you spent more time there than originally planned?

_____

_____

_____

CHAPTER 11

A Spiritual Tune-Up in the Wilderness

Have you ever watched a mechanic or someone working on a car perform a tune-up? Depending on the mileage of a vehicle, there is a checklist of items they need to do to call the job complete. Watching them perform the steps involved looks intense if you're not a mechanic, but I'm sure they do it with ease because of their skillset, and hopefully, because they love what they do.

Watching them get to those hard-to-reach places with a little turn here and a little turn there, using just the right tool is quite artful. For major jobs, they know how to totally dismantle the area they are working on to repair or rebuild it. As part of their final inspection, they ensure that all nuts and bolts are securely in place before turning the vehicle back over to us to pay for their services. Whether the car was taken to the shop for its regularly scheduled maintenance tune-up, or due to sluggish "pick-up" that caused us to schedule the tune-up, it gets done. This scenario made me think about the tuning up of our spiritual lives that often happens in the wilderness.

Unlike periodic scheduled maintenance checks (or something happening that makes us run to God), we should have regular checks with God through our daily worship time. During this time, we connect with Him and get "tuned" in for the day. It sets our path. It sets our focus. Sometimes we may feel a spiritual sluggishness and need to be refreshed, recharged and rejuvenated. There is no better way to get that than by spending time with God and allowing Him to set the course, which could mean fine-tuning some areas.

The God of the universe knows exactly what needs to be done to give us what we need. As surely as we imagine a mechanic under the hood, working so intensely in those tight, hard to reach places, our God, in all His splendor and all His knowledge, knows how to give us the spiritual tune up we need and just when we need it, even in those hard-to-reach places, if we let Him. Once we agree to the change, He meticulously does a little twist and turn here, a little twist and turn there; a removal here and a replacement there; a consistent changing of our oil to keep our engines running smooth and the lamp burning within; and so much more. It's called "change." It's called "adjustments."

No fancy tools are needed. He has one tool, His Word. He is very creative because He is the Creator! We don't have to schedule an appointment because He can help more than one person at the same time in any location, state, or country because of His omnipresence. His "shop" is open 24/7, and we don't need a phone or any electronic device to reach Him. We don't have to search for a specialty shop because He specializes in everything. The cost is doing it His way.

During some of my wilderness moments with a loving Father that led to my spiritual tune-up while going through the process, I learned to:

> Hope again because hope deferred makes the heart sick.
>
> Trust God for everything.
>
> Forgive.
>
> Love.
>
> See things differently.

During this tune-up process our faith is ignited. We learn to trust and obey. We gain the courage to face other challenges, and engage in proper spiritual warfare to fight the real enemy of our soul. What appears to be a set-back in our eyes is a set-up with God. I'm sure Moses and the Israelites thought about that as they were heading in the direction of the wilderness in the Book of Exodus. Even though the Lord was a pillar of cloud by day and fire by night, which was assurance that He was with them, protecting them and guiding them, I'm sure they had concerns when they heard the enemy behind them, saw mountains on both sides of them, and saw a body of water before them.

Trust requires faith, and faith requires action. Part of developing our trust is to understand that when God speaks and makes a promise, there will be a fulfillment of it (see Luke 1:45). At that moment, we need to decide whether to trust Him or not. God may even give a vision of the promise without sharing the path we will need to take to receive it. I believe that is intentional because God knows that if we saw what we may have to go through for the promise to be fulfilled, some of us may decide that we don't want to go that route, missing opportunities or connections along the way.

> "[20] *I have been crucified with Christ [that is, in Him I have shared His crucifixion]; it is no longer I who live, but Christ lives in me. The life I now live in the body I live by faith [by adhering to, relying on, and completely trusting] in the Son of God, who loved me and gave Himself up for me."*
> (Galatians 2:20 AMP)

> "[19-21] *What actually took place is this: I tried keeping rules and working my head off to please God, and it didn't work. So I quit being a "law man" so that I could be God's man. Christ's life showed me how, and enabled me to do it. I identified myself completely with him. Indeed, I have been crucified with Christ. My ego is no longer central. It is no longer important that I appear righteous before you or have your good opinion, and I am no longer driven to impress God. Christ lives in me. The life you see me living is not "mine," but it is lived by faith in the Son of God, who loved me and gave himself for me. I am not going to go back on that. Is it not clear to you that to go back to that old rule-keeping, peer-pleasing religion would be an abandonment of everything personal and free in my relationship with God? I refuse to do that, to repudiate God's grace. If a living relationship with God could come by rule-keeping, then Christ died unnecessarily."*
> (Galatians 2:19-21 MSG)

Now I understand the phrase, "dying to live and losing to gain." It almost seems to be an oxymoron but it's really not. Dying to live is crucifying our fleshly desires to truly live out the Lord's purpose. Losing to gain is giving up the things He says that we might live out our purpose. It's running the race without weights to hold us back.

It's a natural reaction for us to want to see the replacement before we let go of something, but to whom much is given, much is required (Luke 12:48). When I said "yes" to the flesh death, I realized that there is a high cost to following Him and to be His disciple. It's easy to voice it but it's difficult to follow it. To escape my Egypt, the place of my bondage, I had to cross my Red Sea, but I knew I was not going to do it alone.

The wilderness journey and spiritual tune-up in the wilderness make us appreciate things we take for granted. It's hard to appreciate water until you're thirsty. It's hard to appreciate food until you're hungry. It's hard to appreciate light until you've been in darkness. It's hard to appreciate having until you've suffered lack. I've learned to appreciate small things and big things; and I know He's not finished with me yet.

A Moment to Reflect:

What spiritual tune-ups have you experienced in the wilderness?

_____

_____

_____

Would you say that you had to stay in the "soul shop" a little longer for your spiritual tune-up due to disobedience?

_____

_____

_____

What did you learn to appreciate after completely coming out of the wilderness and getting the tune-ups?

_____

_____

_____

CHAPTER 12
Take the Plunge

When we visit an optometrist, the one we often refer to as an eye doctor, for our annual check-ups, we are taken through several routine tests. We look through machines as they flash pictures before us so we can read the lettering or symbols. If they see us struggling, they adjust the dials on the machines to try to make the letters a little clearer, by bringing them closer or further away, as they say, "Try it now. Is that better?"

Based on the results of the exam, we may need to fix a problem with our sight. It could be through corrective lenses worn on the face in the form of eyeglasses, or contact lenses placed directly on the surface of the eye. In some cases, surgery may be needed. Depending on the diagnosis, with the eyeglasses, contact lenses or surgery, our vision is usually restored.

At some point in our lifetime, we've heard or will hear someone speak about vision and purpose. In most cases we hear the terms related as a hand relates to a glove. When we hear it, something normally comes out about the sight because it's hard to understand our purpose without vision, and it's hard to see without knowing our purpose. There must be a personal decision to want the vision beyond what we can see in the natural at the moment. Often, it looks unachievable or impossible. But if we believe, all things are possible (Mark 9:23).

To see what God has in store for us, He will sometimes lead us out of a place and instruct us to lift up our eyes and look ahead. The looking ahead is so we can see the greatness, the depth, and the expansion that He has for us. As we're led from the darkness into the light, He corrects our distorted view, our blurry vision, and our blinded eyes. He shows us the good things He has in store for us by correcting our focus, if we want it.

God gives all of this to us without a visit to the optometrist and without the purchase of eyeglasses, contact lenses or eye surgery. God's corrective lenses are given to us through the promises in His word.

For me to get to the things He was showing me, I had to be willing to do it His way and take the plunge. An illustrative example is from a dream I had several years ago. I was standing in line with several others, waiting to jump off a diving board that was pretty high up. I was fine as long as I was in line chit-chatting and waiting; however, when it was my turn, suddenly, it was not fun anymore. It didn't seem as high when I was behind others; however, when I looked down all I noticed was how high up I was and the pool of water in the deep end that I knew was way above my head. The line was moving fast until it was my turn to take the dive and it came to a sudden halt.

Paralyzed by the fear of jumping, all I could hear behind me were upset people, shouting things like, "Will you go ahead and jump already." "Lady, go ahead and jump." "Move it, will you." "Come on lady, go ahead and jump." The more they shouted, the more I was frozen in my fears, unable to move. I couldn't see beyond the height of the board and the depth of the water. All kinds of thoughts were going through my head including, "Why in the world were you in this line?" There were no friends cheering me on; only a line of upset shouters.

Finally, out of nowhere, someone pushed me and down I went into the water. There was nothing to do but take the plunge. I remember a lifeguard on the side of the pool with a whistle but nothing else as I was taking the plunge. I was surrounded by clear, pool water, and then something absolutely amazing happened. With buoyancy, I bounced back to the top, paddling lightly and the crowd that was once angry and shouting was now cheering. I made it and the water did not overtake me. All I had to do was be willing to take the plunge. In this dream, I was pushed in because fear had gripped me; however, I'm hoping that will not be my life story as I continue to walk this out with the Lord.

If you are one who is struggling with vision and unable to see the purpose God has planned for your life, perhaps you need His corrective vision approach and a little shove off the diving board, unless you're willing to jump on in.

A Moment to Reflect:

Do you feel that you hear from the Lord and keep the vision from Him before you? Why or why not?

_____

_____

_____

Do you think that your vision is distorted sometimes? If so, what do you think could be causing it?

_____

_____

_____

Do you feel you're one who may need a little push off the diving board? Why or why not?

_____

_____

_____

CHAPTER 13

The Mountaintop Experience

Isn't it interesting that sometimes you have to take the plunge before you can get to the top? The climb to the top to see things from a different point of view will change your current perspective and give new vision. I believe so many times, just as God did with Abraham, He will take us to an elevation level to see our promised land so that we stay encouraged along the way. (Genesis 13:14-17)

After publishing my first book and several years before penning this one, I had a dream of what I refer to as "ditching everything that would make sense to climb to the top." In the dream, the location was a familiar main highway near my residence that can become extremely busy at times. It's a flat highway but also a very scenic route of you take it out headed West. In this dream I had just pulled out of a gas station as snow began to lightly fall. The road that is normally flat had a slight incline in the dream. I traveled in a sport utility vehicle (SUV) which was familiar to me because I really owned it. This all-wheel drive SUV could handle snow extremely well.

Although it wasn't blustery in the dream, the snow was beginning to stick to the highway. As the snow continued to fall, I made my way up the incline that seemed to get steeper. Cars and trucks of all shapes and sizes were getting stuck and stopping but I continued to make my way up. I looked back but no one was following me. The other drivers were standing outside of their cars, looking at the snow falling, and sticking, and talking amongst themselves. Their cars and trucks should have been able to make it up the incline, but no longer could.

I glanced back and then forward and kept going until finally, my SUV started slipping as well, which never happened before. I got out of the SUV, looked at the people still standing around with their stalled cars down the hill and started walking up the inclined highway. I started to lose grip but that didn't stop me. I continued the climb. Though I was slipping and my knees were getting scraped, I continued the climb with determination. It seemed each time I would look for anything to grab on to, a twig or something would spring up out of the highway and give me the boost I needed to keep climbing.

You and I know that in the natural, a twig or small growth popping up out of the cracks in the highway could not hold the weight of a human to allow them to pull their weight on it to boost them up, but I believe this was supernatural. It was the help sent from the Holy Spirit because I was determined to make it up the hill. Everything that should have been able to get up the hill, such as my SUV, let me down. The others who were trying to get up the hill stopped climbing. No one was helping anyone, not even to push a car out of the way. I was determined to make it to the top with snow falling heavier. I climbed and climbed, accepting each twig or natural element that popped out of the tarred road. I finally made it to the top and the view was breathtaking. Then I woke up.

This is what our journey to freedom will feel like at times, a solo climb. All those who started off with you may stop. Help that you thought would be able to weather the storm may cut out on you. We may get a little scraped up but we will continue the climb. Our determination and drive to get to where the Lord is trying to take us will cause God's "super" to be added to the "natural" to give us the grip and encouragement we need to keep going. There will be times we will have to step out of what seems normal, and with determination, make the climb, leaving all behind.

Now, I'm not typically a person who loves snow because I associate it with cold weather. Need I say more? However, the snow in the dream represented something. Once I got to the top, it seemed the snow stopped, yet things were covered with the freshness of snow. I could now see clearly after making that climb. Now that I've arrived at the mountaintop, what's next? Since my spiritual sight had changed, I would guess that some shifts from the norm were about to occur. In other words, my plans (again, my plans) were about to be interrupted. Something was shifting to get to the new view He was showing me.

When a shift occurs in the natural it means that something moved from one position to another. Just think about an earthquake or any other natural disaster. Foundational structures are often altered or moved from their original position or they have shifted from its normal state. This sometimes results in unplanned damages to the original structure or even to the foundation that was once thought to be solid. Some structural damages can even go undiscovered for a while. If repairs are needed, they can often be costly and urgent so no further damages are done to persons or to the structure itself.

A spiritual shift is not a bad thing. It's actually coming into agreement with God to accept His will for our life. It reminds me of the passage in 2 Samuel 7 when David was told that his son would build a house for the Lord instead of him. Even though David wanted to, and even though David's heart was in the right place to do it, he accepted God's plan (verse 25). When we pray His perfect will to be done in our life, we then can become a part of His perfect plan for our life.

The season of shifting is not something we should fear once we reach our mountaintop. As Christians, even if it includes a structural change or the existing foundation being ripped up, it should be something we embrace if we're expected to be lined up with our purpose. Maybe the real question is, "Can we handle the shift when our plan is interrupted?"

He may still be asking many of us that same question. He's shown us the new vision that is going to require us to leave a place of comfort. We must step boldly out of the boat to pursue the promise spoken by God (more on this in Chapter 15). This can be scary at times. Things may get rough. Some family members will think we've lost our mind.

Friends may be nowhere to be found. The naysayers will consistently speak negative words against this mountaintop vision. If we focus on all of that, the God-given vision will seem harder to reach.

How many times have we been shown the vision and reasoned with God about it? How often have we settled for the lesser because of our current circumstances? What opportunities are we missing because we decided to focus our attention on the commotion around us? When will we stop limiting a limitless, uncontainable GOD who knows everything about us! Spiritually taking the plunge, and the climb, by way of dreams, probably helped me understand spiritual pregnancies.

A Moment to Reflect:

Are you ready to take that climb with the Lord?

_____

_____

_____

What are you willing to ditch along the way to allow the supernatural to take place?

_____

_____

_____

What has God shown you or spoken to you that is so large that it seems impossible given your current circumstances?

_____

_____

_____

CHAPTER 14

Pregnant with a Promise

Several years ago I had a dream in which I was pregnant. I was in the labor and delivery room, obviously to give birth, except no one was doing anything. There was a doctor and nurse with me; however, they didn't seem to be in a hurry to prep me. They said I was not ready. In other words, what typically happens before a baby is ready to crown had not happened. My water had not broken, and I had not dilated enough (or not at all).

I believe that's what they were seeing in the natural, but it was not what I was feeling at the time. If that were true, I would not have been in labor and delivery. I prepped myself while the medical staff totally ignored my actions. They continued casual dialogue with each other and reviewing charts. I put my feet in the stirrups, hoping they would get in position for the delivery, but still there was no assistance from either of them. They simply were not moved by what I was doing.

I got out of the bed, went by a window and began praying intensely. I saw them peek up from under their glasses away from the charts as if thinking, "She has really lost her mind." They looked at each other as though I was "touched." Then suddenly the nurse glanced at the bed. She saw a water spot on the sheets. She said, "Oh my goodness. Your water did break. Get back in the bed!" Only then did they quickly get in position. They could not perceive the spiritual evidence, but they saw the evidence of readiness in the natural. I casually walked back over to the bed and said, "I told you so." Thank God I had already prepped myself! That was the dream.

Here is a thought to ponder: Before getting in position, there had to be something happening during the waiting. Each of us will have our own stories to tell here. Imagine Mary in Luke 1, chosen to carry Jesus, our Savior, the Holy One. Just as Mary was, we are pregnant with promises from a conception that came from a seed planted by God. He nourishes with His Word as we carry it until it's time to give birth. During the time of waiting, all the pieces are being put firmly in place by the Father of the seed. We begin to see things differently. He gives us a new outlook, a new view. Then, He leads us to the delivery room to birth what's been growing and developing in us over a time period.

If we are not careful, we can abort those seeds of promise because we forget about them. One day while taking a very relaxing walk, the Lord began speaking to me about vision. It was perfect timing because what I didn't realize was that while I was walking, I was looking down. I wasn't looking down for any reason other than just to watch my steps, at least that's what I thought. However, ever so gently the Lord brought it to my attention by simply saying, "Hold your head up. The view is different when you look up."

> "[14] *And the Lord said to Abram, after Lot had separated from him: 'Lift your eyes now and look from the place where you are—northward, southward, eastward, and westward; 15 for all the land which you see I give to you and your descendants[b] forever. [17] Arise, walk in the land through its length and its width, for I give it to you.'"*
> (Genesis 13:14-15, 17)

Oh, how true that statement is. Life can cause us to forget about the seeds He placed inside of us, and we forget to nurture them until it's time to give birth. If we're walking and looking down, we can't see what's before us, even with our peripheral vision. After that, He continued directing my steps, telling me various directions to turn on the open path until I found myself looking out over a horizon, just as Abraham had done in the verses above. He reminded me about vision to not just see what was before me but also beyond what I could not see so I could nurture what He planted inside of me to carry the promise to full-term and not terminate the pregnancy.

I've had many encounters with the Lord, but that encounter caused me to go home and make some changes in my natural environment. I put things before me that reminded me of the promises God had spoken to me so I could capture the vision. I posted scriptures, hung pictures and placed magazines all around me to help me stay focused and see my future the way God saw it. I guess you could call it the start of my vision board, which is another great way to capture God's story for our life and keep it before us. With vision before us, we can agree on earth as it is in Heaven with our prayers and protect His promises in us.

A Moment to Reflect:

Do you feel pregnant and ready to birth something for the Lord?

_____

_____

_____

Do you have the vision of the Lord in view so you can be reminded of it?

_____

_____

_____

Are you willing to allow God to change you to align with the new vision shown and shift you into your purpose?

_____

_____

_____

CHAPTER 15
The Other Side of Through

After making the decision to be free, I began to see things differently. It was a process and it's still unfolding; however, I can now see the vision more clearly. There was one common piece missing each time I could see the end. It was the piece in the middle. It's what I refer to as my own wilderness experience to get to the other side. In addition, I had no indication of the length of the journey because in many cases I was taking the scenic route, as described in Chapter 10. I only knew that I wanted to get there, and the only way to do that was with the Lord.

There were many times while on the journey that I thought, "Dear God, where are You?" But He reminded me that no matter what winds and waves are raging around, there was a promise in His Word that He would never leave nor forsake me if I kept my focus on Him and always stepped in the footprints He already laid out for me. Two scriptures come to mind with this.

"³⁵On the same day, when evening had come, He said to them, 'Let us cross over to the other side.' ³⁶Now when they had left the multitude, they took Him along in the boat as He was. And other little boats were also with Him. ³⁷And a great windstorm arose, and the waves beat into the boat, so that it was already filling. ³⁸But He was in the stern, asleep on a pillow. And they awoke Him and said to Him, 'Teacher, do You not care that we are perishing?' ³⁹Then He arose and rebuked the wind, and said to the sea, 'Peace, be still!' And the wind ceased and there was a great calm. ⁴⁰But He said to them, 'Why are you so fearful? How is it that you have no faith?' ⁴¹And they feared exceedingly, and said to one another, 'Who can this be, that even the wind and the sea obey Him!'"

(Mark 4:35-41)

"²²Now it happened, on a certain day, that He got into a boat with His disciples. And He said to them, 'Let us cross over to the other side of the lake.' And they launched out. ²³But as they sailed He fell asleep. And a windstorm came down on the lake, and they were filling with water, and were in jeopardy. ²⁴And they came to Him and awoke Him, saying, 'Master, Master, we are perishing!' Then He arose and rebuked the wind and the raging of the water. And they ceased, and there was a calm. ²⁵But He said to them, 'Where is your faith?' And they were afraid, and marveled, saying to one another, 'Who can this be? For He commands even the winds and water, and they obey Him!'"

(Luke 8:22-25)

Allow me to set the scene. Jesus is the One with the suggestion to cross over to the other side of the lake. He and His disciples left the multitude and launched out to sail. Would you agree that sometimes we may need to leave the crowd to cross over into something new? While trying to follow Jesus (the Word), the waves started beating. Can you relate to this?

We have to love Jesus' style. What is there not to love? He is purposeful because He knows His purpose. He has His actions for the day because He already met with His Father about them. Why would we not want to hang out with Jesus as He surely knows where He's going!

Picture this in light of the passages. Jesus made the suggestion to cross over to the other side. He had to know about the entire journey over; however, He failed to share one very important piece of information. Yes! A windstorm was coming, the waves would beat into the boat and the boat would start filling with water. But, hey, there's nothing to panic about. Jesus is on board.

One might think having that piece of information beforehand would have prepared the disciples for what was about to happen, but that may not be the case. Why? Because just hearing that small, yet important, relevant piece of information probably would have left some with decisions to make, such as, whether or not to follow. That would have been the question. After all, we depend on the weather channels and meteorologists to help us decide whether or not to go on cruises, to sail, to fish or participate in any other activities involving large bodies of water.

Therefore, not thinking anything strange about the request and wanting to follow Jesus, they pile into the boat. The rest of the story unfolds. What is Jesus doing? He is asleep! But Jesus calmly gets up after being frantically awakened by the panicking disciples, speaks to the wind and the sea and suddenly, there was calm. Just like that. To top it off, He turns to the disciples and addresses their fears. Whose idea was it anyway to cross over to the other side? Our next assignment or opportunity could be waiting there. He promised never to leave nor forsake us if we follow Him. Why not get in the boat and cross over to the over side?

There may be times when we feel we're being hit on all sides because we decided to cross-over. The water has filled the boat. We may feel we are drowning. We can feel the oppressiveness of the opposition all around us. Everything may appear to be chaotic and in turmoil, yet in the midst of it all, in the very center, is the Leader, the One who suggested crossing over. He is asleep in the stern of the boat. While the windstorm is swirling around, it's hard to focus on the promise that He will never leave us nor forsake us. However, it is as if the Father is saying, "Rest. Get some sleep because I have this." That is trust.

The disciples walked with and could see, feel and touch Jesus. Though He was physically present with them in the boat, they asked a question we might ask. "How can you just watch me/us go through this and not come to my/our rescue?" He responded by not only addressing the situation but also questioning their lack of faith.

Perhaps Jesus was thinking, "You have spent some time with Me. You heard some of My teachings. You witnessed some healings. You have some indication of Who is in the boat with you and yet, you don't trust Me though it was my suggestion to cross over to the other side." If He suggested it, then everything must be in order. If we stay with Him and do what He tells us, then things are already in order.

Many of us may be familiar with the poem entitled "Footprints In the Sand" (Stevenson, copyright 1984). The message is about a rough period in the author's life when he thought the Lord had abandoned him because he saw only one set of footprints in the sand where there had been two sets. The Lord responded by saying that it was during the rough times that He had carried him.

One day several years ago, during my worship time, the Lord gave me another meaning that was personally for me. It happened during the time of surrendering from my way of doing things to follow Him so that I might walk in my purpose to reach my destiny. The Lord shared with me that if I'm truly following Him, I should see only one set of footprints because He has already gone before me to make the way. He was telling me to firmly place my feet in the set of footprints He had already walked, not stepping off to the right or left. If I do that, I'll never be off course.

If I'm stepping in His set of footprints, I'm always following the Light. Imagine for a moment that you're in a pitch-black room. If you've ever been in a pitch-black room, you already know that you can't see a thing. It's not a good feeling. Not only can you not see anything around you, you don't know where you're stepping, who or what things are in there with you, or in which direction to go.

I believe one of the first things anyone would do if they found themselves in a room like this is look for light, any speck of light. Even if there is only a small pinhole of light, it still means there is something bright on the other side. It would lead us to believe there is an opening somewhere. It would help us stand on faith believing there is a way out! According to Psalm 119:105, the Word of God is our light. It lights our path to give us the right amount of light to see where we're going. It lights our path to give direction.

It's time for many of the God's children to launch. It's time to cross over to the other side. Isn't it comforting to know that we can rest on the journey because our Father has everything under control? This journey we are on with the Lord is not about us. There are connections we need to make along the way to be a blessing to others as others are waiting to bless us. We have permission to use the authority He's given us. To the winds and the waves swirling around us we can say, "Peace be still because I'm crossing over." We can rest in the assurance that He is with us. We can fluff our pillows up in the stern of the boat too. Even if the "boat" is filling up with water and we feel we are drowning or about to drown, we can say, "Peace be still."

While crossing over from a place of bondage, the children of Israel feared the same way the disciples feared.

> *"[10]And when Pharaoh drew near, the children of Israel lifted their eyes, and behold, the Egyptians marched after them. So they were very afraid, and the children of Israel cried out to the LORD. [11]Then they said to Moses, 'Because there were no graves in Egypt, have you taken us away to die in the wilderness? Why have you so dealt with us, to bring us up out of Egypt? [12]Is this not the word that we told you in Egypt, saying, "Let us alone that we may serve the Egyptians?" For it would have been better for us to serve the Egyptians than that we should die in the wilderness.' And Moses said to the people, '[14]The LORD will fight for you, and you shall hold your peace.' [15]And the LORD said to Moses, 'Why do you cry to Me? Tell the children of Israel to go forward.'"*
> (Exodus 14:10-15)

When He tells us to go forward, we must know that He is leading us safely to the other side. A thought to ponder, would it be better to stay enslaved and in bondage or trust the Lord when He says it's time to move?

A Moment to Reflect:

Are you ready to cross over to the other side with the Lord without knowing the elements you might face along the way in blind faith?

_____

_____

_____

Have you ever felt as the disciples did in the boat, crying out, wondering why the Lord was asleep? Describe how you felt. What are some things you prayed? How did the Lord respond?

_____

_____

_____

Is there a time when you can say you placed your feet in the prints already made by the Lord to go to the other side?

_____

_____

_____

CHAPTER 16
Sweet Surrender

You can tell by now that I dream and see visions a lot. Here is another one for you. I was praying several years ago about many things going on. You might say I was crying out to the Lord again, pleading for help. During my time of supplication, I had a vision.

I was in a vehicle in the driver's seat. I scooted over just a little and patted the seat (the itty-bitty room I left, not quite half) for the Lord to sit down. In other words, I was saying to Him, I want you to help but I don't want to get out of the driver's seat because I still want to be somewhat in control of the situation. I want to be sure of the path You are going to take me down because I might not want to go that route. That was evidence of the huge trust issue I had with the Lord.

Imagine that. Offering the Lord a partial seat as I was asking for His help instead of moving all the way over to the passenger side and saying, "Lord, You take the wheel and I'll go along for the ride." I had to laugh at myself after I saw that vision. If we learn to stop and listen to the response when we are praying, we could hear God simply say, "I have this, just scoot over."

I learned a valuable lesson about wanting to do things alone while watching a two-year-old eat his breakfast one morning. Filled with morning joy, he sat there with his miniature spoon in hand ready to go. I noticed that every time a spoonful of applesauce was making its way to his mouth, the spoon was slowly rotating to a downward position and the applesauce would spill off before he got it to his mouth. He would watch it fall and still put the spoon in his mouth, tasting just the small residue that remained on it. He would do it again and again.

I thought it would be kind to help guide his hand as the spoon was traveling to his mouth. To my surprise, without looking at me, he kept his eyes on his spoonful of applesauce and used his other hand to push mine out of the way, as if saying "I have this!"

We're taught to let them feed themselves at that age because that's how they learn. As I watched the applesauce fall off again and again, he continued to turn the spoon as it was making its way to his mouth. More landed on him and his seat than went in his mouth. He was making a real mess. After about four rounds of that, I guess he decided enough was enough, and he moved on to eat the finger foods on his plate.

Laughing (without letting him see me laugh), I let a few minutes pass and then I took the spoon. Playing the childhood "choo-choo train eating game," I fed him a spoonful of applesauce, and he joyfully ate all of it! Afterward, I cleaned up him and his mess, and he left the table full and happy.

I thought about how we sometimes act with God, being so independent and rushing. We hold our miniature spoon, pushing away help and assistance from Him because "we have it." God, being the loving parent that He is, just stands back watching us make the biggest mess ever. We try repeatedly until we decide that enough is enough. In the midst of our tears and mess, He's there to wipe our face, clean off our hands and clean up our mess. What an awesome and loving God!

A lesson to learn here is that when we pray and ask God for assistance, He really does "have it." We don't have to struggle with a small, miniature spoon. He has the right tools! If we take our hands completely off the steering wheel and get out of the driver's seat, He will lead and guide us. There will be no messes or clean ups after because truly, "He has it!" Oh, the lessons of a two-year old.

"Just let go and let God." It's a phrase we use all the time. It just seems to roll out naturally. But do we really understand what it means to completely let go and let God have His way? Do we continue to want to hold on to just a piece of whatever it is?

In my walk with the Lord, especially after making so many messes, I now know that making a statement like that is not to be taken lightly. Something truly happens as a result of letting go that changes the course of situations for the best. It is His will that is done and not my own.

A faithful and loving God will do exactly what He promised. The key is letting go and relinquishing complete control to Him. When we let go by taking our hands off the entire matter, He is free to handle it the way He chooses, and we have peace.

A Moment to Reflect:

Have you ever prayed about something, and didn't completely surrender it over to the Lord to handle? If so, provide at least one example.

_____

_____

_____

What happened as a result of not completely letting go?

_____

_____

_____

Are at a place of complete surrender, partial surrender or still struggling with the word surrender? Whatever the answer, explain why you answered that way.

_____

_____

_____

CHAPTER 17
The Dance

In most traditional wedding ceremonies, the bride is escorted arm-in-arm down the aisle by her father or by someone asked to stand in her father's stead to give her away. After they arrive at the altar, the minister or person presiding over the wedding will say something like, "Who gives this woman to this man?" The father, or the designee, will proudly say, "I do." Then the escort of the bride gently breaks away and places her hand on the hand of the anxiously awaiting groom. She steps forward into position next to her soon-to-be-husband as the ceremony continues. The father takes his seat.

The words "I do" mean so much in a wedding ceremony. Not only are they spoken when the father responds to the question to give the bride away, but the words are usually used by the bride and the groom as the wedding vows are read. Both the bride and groom say "I do" acknowledging that they agree with the question asked. Her life is no longer her own. His life is no longer his own. The father, or designated stand-in, gave her to the groom to love her, care for her, honor her, provide for her, along with other actions mentioned in the wedding vows. During the exchange of vows, both promise to love, honor and cherish each other until they die.

God showed me something so beautiful using William McDowell's song, "I Give Myself Away" on his *As We Worship* album. He showed me a wedding ceremony. This time, a person, not gender specific, was walking by themselves with no escort. They calmly walked down the long aisle with a smile on their face. When they reached the foot of the altar, a gentle voice came out of nowhere. There was no minister or person presiding over the ceremony. It was a personal decision. It was a personal ceremony. It was a personal choice. The voice asked, "Who gives this man or woman to Me?" The person at the altar replied, "I do. I give myself away, so You can use me." Wow! What a beautiful vision.

I reflected on some of the lyrics in the song. "I give myself away, so You can use me." And then, "My life is not my own, to You I belong. I give myself, I give myself to You." I looked at that in a couple of ways. First, for those who have never given their lives to Jesus and would like to become a part of the real family, it's a new beginning. Second, for those of us who have already given our lives to Jesus, and are ready to give Him total control of every area in our lives, we, too, give ourselves away.

When we make a decision to give ourselves to Jesus, it's a walk we take by ourselves because it's a personal decision. We place our hands in His because we trust Him. By God's word, He promises to take care of us. It's simple. We don't have to look for Mr. or Ms. Right, because He is it. We don't have to date a long time and hope that one day we'll start talking marriage. We don't have to wait for a formal proposal because it's an open invitation. All He wants is a repentant, open heart to receive Him.

Many of us have heard of the term "DUI" which refers to driving under the influence of some controlled substance. Under the influence of someone or something, they or it can take control of our mind. Our thought life can become so clouded to the point we no longer make the right decisions. We are not thinking clearly.

That's why we're warned of substances that are intoxicating, and narcotics that alter our thinking. We're warned not to operate machinery or drive while taking certain medications as one of the side effects could be drowsiness. Driving under the influence can cause serious consequences.

But there is an influence that is perfectly alright to be under and that is the influence of the Holy Spirit. Under the influence of the Spirit, we are so full of the Spirit of God in us through Jesus Christ that our flesh is no longer in control. Galatians 5:25 says, "If we live in the Spirit, let us also walk in the Spirit." Under His influence, the Holy Spirit will lead and guide us in everything we have to do. He will lead and guide us in decisions. His way then becomes our way, His desire becomes our desire, and His purpose becomes our purpose.

Some of us will often quote a well-known passage in the Bible located in Psalm 37:4, "Delight yourself also in the Lord, and He shall give you the desires of your heart." When our desires are those that come from the Lord, He will fulfill them because it's no longer what we want that's in our heart. It's what He wants that will be in our heart, and it is what He will give us.

When we say "I do" and give ourselves away to Him, there is a different kind of influence controlling us. It's the influence of the Holy Spirit. Under His influence, everywhere we go, everyone we come in contact with, and every decision we make, will be because the Holy Spirit led the way. The only consequence of that is the promise of His blessing in the Word of God, so we can't go wrong or lose with that.

This kind of love, this kind of influence is overwhelming. This is the dance that I want to last forever. I want to dance every step and every tune with my only partner, God! I don't want this dance to be the last one with Him because I want to dance with Him forever, and this time, I want Him to lead. He is one Partner who will never leave me solo on the dance floor, nor reject me when I ask for the dance; nor do I want to reject Him. This is just the beginning of our love relationship that will never end.

A Moment to Reflect:

Describe how the illustration of the wedding ceremony spoke to you.

_____

_____

_____

Have you given yourself away to be completely used by the Lord? Why or why not?

_____

_____

_____

Do you have additional areas in your life that you need to surrender to the Lord? If so, name at least one.

_____

_____

_____

CLOSING THOUGHTS

I've wasted time trying to do it my way; wanting to see what the replacement was before I would let go of something I was holding onto. However, there were steps I had to take to receive what the Lord had for me. It's what I call the biblical "if-then" model. It's God Himself saying, "If you will then I will." I realized that I had to remove Band-Aids to allow the wounds to be healed by the Lord. Now God is the wind in my sail, blowing me the way He wants me to go. God is my joy, which produces my strength. God turned my mourning into dancing.

> "The Spirit of the Lord God is upon Me, because the Lord has anointed Me to preach good tidings to the poor; He has sent Me to heal the brokenhearted to proclaim liberty to the captives, and the opening of the prison to those who are bound; ²To proclaim the acceptable year of the Lord, and the day of vengeance of our God; to comfort all who mourn, ³To console those who mourn in Zion, to give them beauty for ashes, the oil of joy for mourning, the garment of praise for the spirit of heaviness; that they may be called trees of righteousness, the planting of the Lord, that He may be glorified." ⁴And they shall rebuild the old ruins, they shall raise up the former desolations, and they shall repair the ruined cities, the desolations of many generations. ⁵Strangers shall stand and feed your flocks, and the sons of the foreigner shall be your plowmen and your vinedressers. ⁶But you shall be named the priests of the Lord, they shall call you the servants of our God. You shall eat the riches of the Gentiles, and in their glory you shall boast. ⁷Instead of your shame you shall have double honor, and instead of confusion they shall rejoice in their portion. Therefore in their land they shall possess double; everlasting joy shall be theirs."
>
> (Isaiah 61:1-7)

Finish the Race

> "Let us lay aside every weight, and the sin which so easily ensnares us, and let us run with endurance the race that is set before us."
> (Hebrews 12:1)

The above verse from the New King James version is probably what most people are familiar with; however, the Message Bible says it this way:

> "Do you see what this means—all these pioneers who blazed the way, all these veterans cheering us on? It means we'd better get on with it. Strip down, start running—and never quit! No extra spiritual fat, no parasitic sins. Keep your eyes on Jesus, who both began and finished this race we're in. Study how he did it. Because he never lost sight of where he was headed—that exhilarating finish in and with God—he could put up with anything along the way: Cross, shame, whatever. And now he's there, in the place of honor, right alongside God. When you find yourselves flagging in your faith, go over that story again, item by item, that long litany of hostility he plowed through. That will shoot adrenaline into your souls!"
> (Hebrews 12:1-3 MSG)

Reading this passage reminded me of a relay race where the baton passes from one person to the next on the same team. Then the Lord pointed out to me that we all have purpose with one common goal, to build His Kingdom. God created every person for a reason, and through Jesus Christ, we will be able to do all things (Philippians 4:13), but we need to get in the race.

I visualized several runners, each in their lane. They were focused on their transition point where the baton would be passed to the next runner or where they would cross the finish line, completing that particular race or assignment.

Imagine the race for a moment. The runner is approaching you. You are getting in position to receive the baton. The crowd is cheering loudly. Even if you feel slightly nervous, it doesn't show because your momentum is building by the cheering crowd. Your turn is coming. You slowly start trotting. When the runner reaches you, you grab the baton and take off. Your adrenaline is pumping. Sweat begins to pour, but your legs are strong. Suddenly, you don't feel tired. Your focus, your concern is to either pass the baton to the next person or burst thru the finish line so you can move on to your next assignment.

Finally, with hands in the air, it's over. You feel a sense of accomplishment. Either you completed that portion and the whole team runs over to celebrate in unity, or you continue cheering your teammates on because the race is still in progress. Your part of that race is finished.

We all have a God-given assignment. Whether we are birthing something totally new or taking part in another race, we must complete our part. Someone is waiting to receive the baton or waiting for us to burst through the ribbon that marks the end of the line for that particular part of our journey before we can move on to the next. This is the vision God gave me.

Life is a race and we each have a part. He who has begun a good work in us will surely complete it (Philippians 1:6), but we must get in the race.

Now we have the responsibility to ask ourselves, "Are we running with endurance so that the next person to receive the baton can take off or are we holding things up? Are we nurturing the dream God impregnated us with until ready for labor and delivery, or are we holding on to it? Is the adrenaline shooting into our soul as described in the passage from the Message Bible, or did we quit before or in the middle of the race? Who is running our race?"

The Decision

Running the race is not possible without a relationship with God through Jesus Christ. Experiencing true freedom is not possible without a relationship with God through Jesus Christ. God knows that we will be hurt in life. He knows we will go through some painful things. He also knows what it will take to heal our wounded heart. He knew from the beginning that it was necessary to restore the relationship between fallen man and Himself. Jesus was sent to live, to die and to be resurrected to restore our relationship with the Father.

It's not too late to enjoy the freedom of being healed of hurts. It's not too late to join the race. God loves you. He loves you so much that He gave His only Son to die so that you can live.

If you're ready to take that walk to give yourself away and dance with the Lord, then I invite you to make some confessions based on your current relationship with God. If you do not have a relationship with God through Jesus Christ or feel that you've walked away from God, then I invite you to pray the Prayer of Salvation. If you are a Christian and desire to let God lead the dance by following His instructions, then I invite you to pray the Prayer of Surrender.

After you've made the decision and prayed, I encourage you, if you don't have a place to grow in your relationship with God, to find a solid Bible-believing, teaching church where you can be nurtured in His Word.

Prayer of Salvation

"If you confess with your mouth the Lord Jesus and believe in your heart that God has raised Him from the dead, you will be saved."
(Romans 10:9)

Lord Jesus, I know that I am a sinner and I ask for Your forgiveness. I believe You are the Son of God who died on the cross for my sins, was buried and rose from the dead. I want to turn from my sins, trust and follow You. I invite You to come into my heart and life as my Lord and Savior. In the Name of Jesus, Amen.

Prayer of Surrender

This is a suggestion only to get you started; however, you are encouraged to pray your own as it pours from your heart or personalize this to make it your own, especially to touch in the areas you are surrendering to the Lord.

> My loving Father, today, I surrender. I invite you to come into my heart, into those secret places so I can be free of anything hindering reaching my destiny. I want to get on board with Your plans and purpose for my life because You know them (Jeremiah 29:11). I'm thankful for the greatest gift I could have ever received, Your Son, Jesus Christ. I claim the victory at Calvary over every area of my life as I willingly surrender to You to have Your way and take the lead, withholding nothing. Thank You Lord for the Holy Spirit leading me in decisions and guiding me on the paths before me. Help me to become the person You created me to be. As I apply Your word daily, I thank You for being faithful to keep Your word by watching over it (Jeremiah 1:12) and not allowing it to return back void (Isaiah 55:8-11). Thank You for forgiveness and cleansing of my sins. I give myself away to be used by You. In the Name of Jesus. Amen.

OTHER PUBLICATIONS

Make This House Into A Home by Karen Portman

The author uses the lyrics of two popular songs and the storyline of a movie to bring to life the real meaning of a home in comparison to how much God loves us and longs to completely renovate us.

Publication Date: 2012; Reprint 2015.
ISBN: 978-0-9964047-1-6
Available on Amazon.

There Will Be A Fulfillment by Karen Portman

This book is for individuals whose vision has been distorted or blinded. Let this book take you on a spiritual journey so that anything blocking your vision will be removed so you can propel forward into your God-given destiny.

Publication Date: May 2015
ISBN: 978-0-9964047-0-9
Available on Amazon.

Practical Truths for Every Day Living by Dr. Peggy Scott

In this book, Dr. Scott shares sound biblical principles that will encourage you to: Push through fears, failures, and mistakes of the past that negatively influence your life choices and affect your decisions you make every day. Challenge old mindsets and take new risks to venture beyond your comfort zone. Step into a new dimension and level of God-consciousness; moving forward in the plan that God has ordained and predestined for your life.

Publication date: 2014
ISBN: 978-0-9830261-1-2
Ebook ISBN: 978-0-9830261-2-9

ABOUT THE AUTHOR

KAREN PORTMAN is a highly sought-after mentor, coach, seminar presenter, and teacher, and she handles it all with humility. It takes one encounter with Karen to realize she is gifted and anointed to do the work God has assigned to her hands. Her unquenchable desire to serve and her boundless energy makes her a formidable talent to harness. She trains and equips. She helps churches start intercessory prayer ministries or train intercessors. She conducts various workshops on emotional healing, vision and purpose, prayer, women's issues, and other topics. She teaches youth, and assists with revivals, while teaching all levels of prophetic classes for Kingdom Building Institute, a virtual school. With a deep compassion to see people saved and fulfilling their destiny, Karen is driven to reach the lost, and to encourage people of all ages to walk in their purpose. When giving of herself, she does not think it robbery to spend time ministering, mentoring or praying.

Although she loves to have details and facts before making a decision, she describes her spiritual walk as "the Abraham journey" as outlined in Genesis 12:1.

> "Now the Lord had said to Abram: 'Get out of your country, from your family and from your father's house, to a land that I will show you.'"

When God speaks, she moves, often not knowing where until God gives the next step. It's walking in the footprints of Jesus.

She is a servant for the Lord and has faithfully: served in ministries teaching children, youth and families; led intercessory prayer ministries; served as a deaconess, as well as in several other ministries. Karen acknowledged her call to preach the Gospel in 2004. She was licensed in 2006 and ordained in 2009 (at previous churches), and afterwards ordained as a prophetess in 2013 under her current leadership. Currently, she is an itinerant minister affiliated with Fellowship Around the Word Church in Franklin, Virginia, and is part of a five-fold leadership ministry.

She believes in cross-pollinating to see the Body of Christ fittingly joined together as one. She is often invited to speak at churches of other denominations, bringing forth the Word of God using the gifts God has blessed her with. She looks for opportunities to share the Word, birth new ideas and incorporate ways in which ministries can work together to grow the Kingdom of God. Her creativity in delivery is cleaver, vibrant, and delightful. She employs an unusual style of first teaching a basic concept, then immediately demonstrating how the information is applied.

Karen is a certified life coach, facilitator, teacher/trainer/equipper, author, and blogger. It's hard to believe there is an ounce of spare time in her life but there is. During those times, she enjoys writing, walking or sitting by the water or at the mountains, volunteering for nonprofit organizations, and fellowshipping with family and friends. She loves traveling, seeing every place she travels to, whether for work or pleasure, as an opportunity to share the Good News of her Lord and Savior, Jesus Christ.

Although Isaiah 61 was the scripture the Lord gave when she accepted her call to ministry, another of her favorite scriptures is found in Isaiah 6:8, "Also I heard the voice of the Lord, saying: 'Whom shall I send, and who will go for Us?' Then I said, 'Here am I! Send me.'"

Karen stands ready to hear God, to obey what He tells her to do and to go where He sends saying, "Here I am, Lord, send me!"

Contact the Author: ksp.author@gmail.com

www.ingramcontent.com/pod-product-compliance
Lightning Source LLC
Chambersburg PA
CBHW071008080526
44587CB00015B/2391